Quintessential Christine

To Tracey

Best wishes

Christine   29/7/2023

Printed in Australia
Cover and internal design by Shawline Publishing Group Pty Ltd

First Printing: July 2023

Shawline Publishing Group Pty Ltd
www.shawlinepublishing.com.au

Paperback ISBN 978-1-9229-9342-7
eBook ISBN 978-1-9229-9354-0

Distributed by Shawline Distribution and Lightning Source Global

 A catalogue record for this work is available from the National Library of Australia

More great Shawline titles can be found by scanning the QR code below.
New titles also available through Books@Home Pty Ltd.
Subscribe today at www.booksathome.com.au or scan the QR code below.

Quintessential Christine

Poems by Christine

Christine would like to dedicate this book of poetry
to her loving family and friends who have been such
a wonderful support throughout her poetic journey.

Contents

Not Fancy

I do not write with fancy words
descriptors that will wow,
instead, my writing's from the heart
with simple thoughts, I allow.
Don't get me wrong, I do admire
those with the flair for prose
or poems written with finesse
where rhyme and meter flow.

I like the little things in life
that are pleasing to my eye,
like dew that forms upon the grass
or a bright sun in the sky.
Smiles from strangers when we pass
just make my day complete
I love a hug and kiss received
from friends I often meet.

I love to read well-written books
a story with a twist,
or poetry, freestyle or rhyme
not many have I missed.
I like to smell the brisk sea breeze
as I walk along the beach,
perhaps collect a shell or two
I find within my reach.

Enjoy the solitude at night
when day has met an end,
relax beside the fireside,
write poetry to send.
We all have something that we like
enjoyment that we've found,
for me it is the simple life
not hard or too profound.

And so, dear friends, from me to you
I hope my words when read
will make you smile, and if you look
you'll see my heart instead.

A Busy Mum

Every day is Mother's Day
we clean, we cook, we sew
costumes, for kids' dress-up play
then out to sport we go.
Cricket, swimming, basketball,
gymnastics, ballet too,
soothe away their tummy aches
as mums, that's what we do.
Get up early, pack their lunch
send them off to school
spick and span with polished shoes
to ensure they learn the rules.
Make their beds, wash their clothes
sometimes put toys away,
help them with their maths homework!
Times tables hear them say.
Bake birthday cakes, their candles light
play pass-the-parcel games,
host sleepovers with friend in tents
of course, you know their names.
Then, through the teen years, drop them off
to parties with their mates,
buy them clothes to keep in style
so they look good on dates.

Give them phones to keep in touch,
but you still foot the bill.
Give driving lessons in your car!
Pay for their license thrill.
Hug them tight when they move out
and hope they'll pass this test,
shed tears on their wedding day
ensure you look your best.
Nurse their newborn baby child
delight in all they do,
proudly look upon your brood
it's all because of you.
Yes, Mother's Day never really ends
each hour a new delight
I would not swap a single one
I think I've got it right.

Sunburnt Country

I love a sunburnt Aussie bloke with great big muscled arms,
His rugged well-built shoulders, and face with all its charms.
I love his thongs and singlet too, and Stubbies shorts, you see,
With his beer gut proudly hanging out, he is the one for me!
I love his Aussie greeting, 'G'day mate' when we meet,
His laugh so loud, make no mistake, you'll know him on
     the street.

I love the Aussie Sheila too; she's really trim and taut
She'll have long legs, tight skirt, great smile, a real good-
     looking sort.
I love her when she's on the beach, bikini-clad and brown,
Or when she meets her friends for lunch, all dressed up for
     the town.
I love the friendly way she says 'G'day mate' when we meet
Her laugh so loud, make no mistake, you'll know her on
     the street.

I love an Aussie BBQ, with chops and snags and steak
And Big Red sauce, a loaf of bread, the salads that we make.
I love the Aussie breakfast time with Vegemite on toast
For Sunday lunch, nothing beats an Aussie dinkum roast.
I love our wine and spirits too, but best is Aussie beer
It's Foster's Gold or Tooheys Blue – you won't find soft
     drinks here.

I love our sport, we watch a lot; of course, we are the best,
We're always fair, we understand, just better than the rest.
I love the Aussie rules we play – that's football, not ping pong
And how the crowds call out real loud if the umpie gets it wrong.
I love the summer tennis too; it's watched by young and old
Or cricket matches the Aussie way, dressed in green and gold.

I love our patriotic style, the anthem that is sung
Advance Australia Fair... I think, don't know the words,
    just hum.
I love our multicultural race, from lands quite near and far,
As a nation proud, we do stand, because that is who we are.
I love the freedom that we have, our wide brown land to roam
This place we call Australia; this place we call our home.

Forget To Remember

My memory is my biggest flaw,
it goes on walkabout.
Forgetting where I've placed my keys,
this makes me run about.
Until they're found, I cannot drive
to where I need to be.
So, search the house from head to toe,
when found, I smile with glee.

I put my glasses down a while,
then wonder where they are.
I cannot read and get quite mad,
they couldn't be too far.
It really wasn't long ago
I took them off my head.
Just where I put them, who would know?
Be careful where I tread.

Sometimes I have a date for lunch
with friends I love to see.
But I've been known to stand them up,
forgetting where to be.
And if I do remember, then
I'll hurry into town
to tell them sorry, please forgive me
my memory's broken down.

I'll drive down to the grocery store,
then park my car to shop.
But when I've got what I came for,
can't find where I did stop.
So, I will walk around, around,
a frown upon my face
until I come across it parked,
right in that carpark space.

I lose my sunnies all the time,
forgot my kids at school.
Did promise that I'd pick them up,
how could I be so cruel?
And all those misdemeanours now,
they'll not let me forget
remind me of the grief they felt,
expect me to regret.

And so, I have a diary now,
to write the time and date.
But I'll forget to read that too,
and so, I'll still be late.
I am not sure if I'll improve
on any given day.
Bad memory is my flaw in life,
I've always been this way.

My Cardboard Cut-Out Husband

I have a brand-new husband
My real one does not know,
I cut him out of cardboard
And have him now for show.

My husband left me months ago
He's living interstate,
His work they came a-begging
And took away my mate.

I've seen him only rarely
It's been six months or more,
So, when his work is finished
I'll greet him, that's for sure.

But meanwhile I've been lonely
And it started out a joke,
Yet now my cardboard cut-out man
Is really a good bloke.

I took him to a party
I dressed him in a suit,
My friends thought that was funny
But told me he was cute.

He sat up at the table
Took his place amongst us all,
And never ate or drank too much
We danced and had a ball.

I sat him in the front seat
To chat while driving on,
He never made a comment
Or told me I was wrong.

At home he does not make a mess
Or belch or let off wind,
His clothes they never need a wash
My real one I may rescind.

When I go out and spend up big
I know he'll never cry,
Because he sits there quietly
When I go out to buy.

The kids they said to me 'Dear Mum
What have you done to Dad?'
But they can see the funny side
Just think that I've gone mad.

So, if my husband stays away
And never does return,
When I get sick of cut-out man
On the fire he will burn.

Then I will make another one
Create a different style,
No permanent arrangement now
Just keep him for a while.

So, to you ladies all out there
Still single or forlorn,
Just make a cardboard cut-out
A new man then reborn.

Head Talk

Head talk, head talk, please just go away,
You come in uninvited and chat with me all day.
Sometimes I want to listen, yet other times do not.
But you just take no notice, and ignore you I cannot.

You keep your idle chatter up, which distracting I do find,
You even interrupt my sleep with thoughts that come to mind.
Your never-ending conversation can become a bore,
But if I need to have a pause, you always just want more.

Occasionally, I'll listen too, a wise word you may speak,
The good advice I'm searching for, from you at times I seek.
And then I smile and think of you with fondness this one time,
'Cause I can then rely on you, be glad that you are mine.

But when you get too busy and just rush around my head,
My temper flares and starts to rise, I'll ignore what you
      have said.
I know I'll never stop this talk; at times, it's almost quiet,
But then some days I wonder if you've started up a riot.

My thoughts become quite scrambled, no sense at all
      they make.
Confusion reigns then in my mind – just what words do I take?
So, sorting out the good from bad, this does become my quest
To find out what you're really like and put you to the test.

Ha, ha, you say, the game is on! as if you have not heard.
I'll challenge you, and then we'll see who'll have the final word.
I know I should not fight with you, my friend you'll always be
As I can never get away, because you're really me.

I wonder then if others have a mind that is not still,
That chats away all day long, to their brain with head talk fill.
Perhaps I am not all alone, there might be others too
That I can ask for sound advice, to tell me what to do.

I've heard that meditation can calm a busy mind
If practiced, daily benefits of stillness I will find.
But time is of the essence, and I always run the clock.
'Slow down,' they say, I know I must, these thoughts I'll
    try to block.

But with you, I will always chat, this is a fact of life.
Yet sometimes when you overtake is when you'll get in strife.
Then I will say, 'Please stop a while, give me a little time.'
And thank the Lord that you have found a word to end
    this rhyme!

A Real Bloke's Shed

Have you ever wondered what's kept in a real bloke's shed?
I bet you thought them full of junk, but I'm telling
    you instead
I've had the privilege to peruse such a shed one night,
It's owned by my mate Kenny, who opened up my eyes.

There was carpet on the floor, compressors by the door,
Nuts and bolts, fishing rods, and Foster's cans galore.
And if you wanted any oil, like sewing, sump, or mower,
Just look around – you'll find it stored, an ice-cream tub's
    the goer.

A pair of boots a little tight he'll fix for future toil,
As Kenny's way to make them fit is dip the toes in oil.
And when I asked, 'What's that you have hidden under wraps?'
'A photocopy machine,' he said, 'and next I need a fax.'

Oh, what delights this shed has brought, all useful stuff
    in here,
Even shiny rolls of foil that hold your cans of beer.
I looked around and then I spied a cot upon the wall
In storage now, he'll pass it on to his eldest son named Paul.

On the shelf, a yellow cage for a bird he may pick up
But have no fear, Jeanette my dear, the feathered kind's enough.
Next to the cage a machine to sew, a little worse for wear
But Ken still keeps it, just in case his overalls might tear.

Equipment plus and flashing stuff in draws all neatly stored,
And tucked away, a paper too, in case you're ever bored.
Although its news has come and gone of what, why, when,
    and how,
This '97 edition's rare, a collector's item now.

However, in this shed, do not smoke, no ashtray can be found
It's tucked away, so if you must, just butt upon the ground.
And for those dark and dismal days when a torch you
    may require,
Ken has several he would lend if ever you enquire.

When talking old but useful parts, yes most still have a spare
In case of breakdowns of the first – of course, that would be rare.
Ken's shed has lots of shi…ny gear, some new, quite fit to hock
But parting with equipment here would give Ken quite a shock.

So, hear now, folks, and listen well – a real bloke's shed has all,
Its contents stored on bench and floor and even up the wall.
And if you ever need a bit of this, or even some of that,
Go to a real bloke's shed; you'll find every piece of crap.

People-Watching

I love to sit and people-watch, to see them come and go,
And wonder where they all come from – I'd really like to know.
Maybe they are off somewhere; what destination's theirs?
I survey them all so thoroughly, with intense and pondered
    stares.

Some walk along with heads down low, their eyes look at
    the ground,
While others stare dead straight ahead, no expression to
    be found.
Then there's those with happy smiles, and conversation flowing
While chatting with a friend or two, their faces all just glowing.

Observe their dress, some really smart, Armani suits impressive,
Or tailored skirts and high-heeled shoes, I know who is
    obsessive.
Or maybe just a casual look, with shorts, a tee, and runners
And kids with caps on back-to-front – that look is for
    the gunners.

And when it gets quite busy too, with people everywhere
My eyes begin to dart about, there's so much to compare.
Sometimes their stories I'll make up, try to work out
    what they do
Enjoy their presence as they near – it's fun, I'm telling you.

I never make a judgement when I see those down and out
But think about their lot in life, hope there is some help about.
Or if I see a grizzly child having tantrums on the run
I try to always keep in mind what it's like to be a mum.

Sometimes they'll look towards my way; I'll smile, and then
    say 'Hi'
Be sure they have no clue about my thoughts as they go by.
For this pastime is my secret, and it's one I do not share
But wonder if there's others too, who people-watch out there.

Home Haircut

'I really need a haircut now,'
I've just heard my son say,
'It has been a very long, long time
I want no more delay.

Locked up here like a prisoner
My hair has surely grown,
A hair appointment I can't make,'
My son began to groan.

'I do not like this shaggy look
You know I keep it short,
My hairdresser, he needs me now,
His wages are just naught.'

I listened to my son, then said,
'I know just what you mean,
I am about to cut my own
Some scissors I have seen.

Into a mirror I will look
Then start first with my fringe,
I'll try my best to cut it straight
If crooked, I'll not whinge.

I'll snip the bits that just stick out
Cut close around my ears,
The back, I will just hack it off,
For this I may need shears.

My store-bought hair dye I'll mix up
To colour up the greys,
Then wash and dry my new hairstyle
And count the money saved.

Attention I will surely get
At me you'll stop and stare,
But know I've saved a fortune
By doing my own hair.

I've practiced on your father too
I've even groomed the dog,
So, with my newfound cutting skills
I think I'll start a blog.

Have put a sign on my front fence
Free Haircuts With a Smile,
However, when the neighbours pass
They seem to run a mile.

So, son, if desperate you become
Please do not hesitate,
Just call in for your home haircut
A new style I'll create.'

Billy Carts And Marbles

Yes, we all played marbles when we were kids,
had a big 'Tom Bowler' and a bag full of migs.
Held onto your marble with fingers and thumbs
no fudging allowed, and your eye was the plumb.
Picked out your opponent and stayed on the line,
connect with a 'kisser' – that marble's now mine!

I also had swappies, a hand full of cards
would take them to school, start bargaining hard.
I'll swap you this, if you swap me that
get a pair or set, so long as they matched.
We all had so many by the end of the day
we'd sort out our stacks, or just put them away.

Outside we played hopscotch, a tor we would find
drew lines on the concrete, or dirt, did not mind.
Threw into the big squares, then hopped up and down
but you were out if your foot touched the ground
or stood on the lines, so we learnt how to leap
right into the squares, not just fall in a heap.

With a billy cart made from pram wheels and wood
collected from tips, we brought home what we could.
Rope we would tie on, to steer the front wheels
attached to the t-bar, we'd brake with our heels.
Then, down the big hill we would really fly fast
and if one fell off, we'd have a good laugh.

On wet days we stayed in and played our boardgames.
Tiddlywinks or Ludo, the boys had their trains.
But often outside in our gumboots we'd go
to play in the rain or build men in the snow.
For hours in raincoats, we'd all ride our bikes,
then if it was windy, release our stringed kites.

A skipping rope featured, and a big hoop
even boys had a go when we looped the loop.
Kiss-chasey when older, to catch out someone
with a peck on the cheek, oh what innocent fun.
Our days always filled, 'I'm bored' never said
up early each morning, then early to bed.

On that bush school I went to, my memories still dwell
the three Rs we learnt there, plus we all could spell.
On Monday mornings, the flag we would raise
singing God Save the Queen, with respect would we praise.
Oh yes, I remember, with fondness recall
those days of my childhood, how we had it all.

Anzac Day, 25th April

Scared sons with guns ran through the sea
Brave soldiers faced the dice.
On Turkish soil, Gallipoli
Too many paid the price.

Mistakes were made, the landing wrong
The Turks they lay in wait.
Commanders gave the order – 'GO!'
So many lost a mate.

In trenches laid in mud and rain
Their hell on earth began.
They learnt to keep their heads below
Or face the sniper's gun.

And so, the ANZAC spirit grew
In sons from southern lands.
Australian and New Zealand troops
United took their stand.

They lived and crawled in trenches deep
Conditions were so bad.
But strength of mateship gave them hope
Each other's backs they had.

For months on end, they struggled on
Their spirits wearied not.
Relentless in their quest to win
Despite so many shot.

A letter from the war received
By mothers of the dead.
While others prayed, 'My son keep safe,'
This letter one would dread.

This savage war came to an end
Back home survivors sailed.
With horrors never talked about
Regrets for those they failed.

And so today we bow our heads
For those we cannot see.
Brave ANZAC boys from World War One
Lost at Gallipoli.

The wreaths all laid, the bugle blows
A silent minute met
A haunting reverence observed
Last Post: Lest We Forget.

Burn For You

Oh yes, my love, I hear your call
Come lie with me and feel my all.
I'll warm your body from the cold
Caress your skin and gently hold.

I know you'll come whenever I say
I'm here again for you to lay.
Stretched out and naked on your bed
Just like two lovers newly wed.

For years I've been your one desire
To warm your heart with burning fire.
To touch your soul is now my quest
And when you smile, I've passed the test.

We touch and mingle and entwine
For I am yours and you are mine.
Connected by a want and need
'Just come again,' I hear you plead.

Now that I'm here, I'll shine for you
To heat your body through and through.
And then I'll whisper in your ear
'I will be back, so never fear.'

I'll not abandon you at will
But many days I must be still.
I'll not come out for days on end
But then appear, a call I'll send.

And so, upon this autumn day
My rays are warm in which you lay.
I hear you say, 'Thanks, lovely one.'
The pleasure's mine – your loving sun.

Flying High

I am not sure about the theme
but this is one I know.
So, I shall write about a dream
I had not long ago,
my pen will let it flow.

It happened when I was asleep
I grew some wings one night.
I flapped them with a great big sweep
soon found I was in flight,
sharp my vision's sight.

And without fear I soared so high
my confidence just grew.
Went up and down throughout the sky
around, around I flew,
so dazzled by the view.

Took off and flew around the world
all countries passed with ease.
Went up and down, I whirled and swirled
over mountains and the seas,
wings fanned by gentle breezes.

However, soon my wings grew weak
and I woke up in bed.
My dream was like a lightning streak
gone in a flash instead,
'twas all just in my head.

Bush Pee

Now! have you ever tried to take a pee?
while squatting down and hiding in the bush.
But first, you pull your jeans and undies down,
while all the time you're showing off your tush.

Grab at your jeans and undies in one hand,
to keep them out the way before you go.
While balanced in a squat, your legs apart
you think you're ready then to let it flow.

But as it starts you know you'll only squirt
it everywhere, except upon the ground.
To late! you realise you cannot stop
pee on your legs, your jeans, and all around.

You'll try to hold it back and change
the position of your squat, that's the plan.
You curse and swear, but then it squirts again
It's times like this you wish you were a man.

They undo their zip and let it all hang out
before they start, just hold it in their hand.
Point and direct the flow to where they want
'cause they can take a pee while they still stand.

But no! me, I need to squat,
on wobbly legs while trying not to fall.
Then as I go, I know I'll wet my pants
but how to stop it, I have bugger all.

So! next time when I am out in the bush,
and need to pee, I'll strip off all my clothes.
I'll stand up straight, pretend I'm a man
and maybe only pee upon my toes.

But wait! I have now found the perfect seat,
that I can use when I need a bush pee.
No longer have to squat and squirt it out,
I'll take my new 'Bush Dunny Seat' with me.

World Nude Gardening Day

Out gardening I was one day
When my husband said,
'You're inappropriately dressed, my dear,
For this special day ahead.

Don't you know what date this is?'
So smugly he did say.
'I've heard it on the radio,
It's World Nude Gardening Day.

Every year, this day is held
First Saturday in May.
So, maybe you should join them too?
Put your body on display.'

I saw him smile, he did not think
That I would have the gall.
So quickly did I go inside
And strip down to my all.

Then stood in all my glory
Out naked in the yard.
He looked at me, and nearly choked
When my clothes I did discard.

What? Never mind the neighbours
'Cause if they glimpse my bum
I'm sure my rude behaviour
Will be seen as just some fun.

My children too may be quite shocked
When this poem I will post.
On Facebook I may find myself blocked
If this spreads coast to coast.

And so today I'm out in style
I hope I don't offend.
For all I'll wear is just a smile
While to my garden I tend.

It Only Took One

There was movement throughout the nation
for the word had passed around
that a viral epidemic was on its way.
Its origins were sketchy, and nobody knew for sure
but they think it maybe started with just one man.
He had eaten something foreign with a germ tucked up inside
then passed this virus on throughout Wuhan.

People started dying, and authorities were told
but decided they'd ignore the warning signs,
until they then got out of hand – this virus soon was spread
to others, who infected fellow man.
Corona was upon us, no boundaries did it have
and soon we saw it reaching other lands.

Cruise ships were contaminated, panic soon took hold
just what were we to do to stop this curse?
With numbers all increasing, the death rate climbing high
it was declared a pandemic, travel banned over the land.
Isolation from the virus, quarantine was put in place
as governments across the globe made plans.

We saw supermarket shelves stripped bare of their produce
as shoppers in their panic stocked up high,
the toilet rolls and soaps were first, next pasta and the rice
this trend was seen right across the world.
Confusion reigned over us, each other we now feared
with social isolation the new words.

No social get-togethers and all sporting venues closed,
many businesses were forced to shut their doors.
Schoolkids told to stay at home with playgrounds out
    of bounds
activities indoors they had to find.
Weddings, though, could go ahead, but guest lists down to five
with funerals, only ten could stand in line.

Yet still we saw some silly folk defying all the rules
they thought somehow the virus they'd escape,
by lying on the beaches, or to parties they would go
where social distance standards they ignored.
Be warned, you foolish people, for after your next sneeze
you may find this virus down those lungs of yours.

Although the rising numbers hurt, one day they will decrease
and Covid-19 will just disappear,
but meanwhile, it is up to us from every walk of life
to mind how very serious this is.
Stay thankful for the help at hand from workers on front lines
who put themselves at risk so we may live.

So yes, our lives have altered, all within a few short weeks
and perhaps will never be the same again
with future plans all put on hold, no choice do we have
but to comply with what the experts say.
Still, keep in mind, a greater force unites us one and all
humanity will see us through each day.

Greatest Love

At last, a chance to write to you and tell you how I feel
Beside you every day I stand, my love now I reveal.
Cradled in your arms at night, with you content to lie
Devilish good looks you have, delicious on the eye.
Endless days of ecstasy, entice me with your charm
Forever in my heart you'll stay, my never-ending calm.
Gentle, kind, and generous, my girlish hopes fulfil
Happy with you by my side, you are my hero still.
In love with you I've always been, I want no other man
Jealousy I've never had, I am your greatest fan.
Knowing that you keep me safe, protector of my soul
Loving you eternally will always be my goal.
Marrying you, I couldn't wait to hear those words: 'I do'
No other man would ever be quite as good as you.
Obsessed, you hold me in your spell, my object of desire
Passionately you kiss my lips; you set my heart on fire.
Quarrels few, get over them quick, our grudges never last
Respect each other's differences, and let the past be past.
Surprise me with your little gifts, send roses every week
Trust in your great wisdom too, for this I'll always seek.
Understanding of my needs, it's me your arms enfold
Vulnerable I never feel, 'cause you keep out the cold.
Walking hand in hand with you, great comfort you provide
X-ray of my soul would find your imprint stamped inside.
You are my everlasting love, my treasured, caring king
Zero do I want or need; you are my everything.

I Hate Ironing

Oh, how I hate the ironing
A chore that I detest,
But I am so pedantic
Must always look my best.

I do not like seeing wrinkles
So, I'll get out my board,
And when my ironing's finished
My ironing skills applaud.

I flatten down the collars
Put creases in the shirts,
I sometimes iron knickers
Put pleats back in my skirts.

I learnt at school to iron
As well as how to starch,
Domestic science goddess
I topped this very class.

But when I finally married
It wasn't in my vows,
To cook or clean or iron
Just happened, I suppose.

My husband made me boxes
To store unironed clothes,
But they soon fill up quickly
The lids get hard to close.

I should be like my daughter
She irons not a thing,
Just washes, hangs, and neatly folds
Straight from the line she'll bring.

I think her clothes are all drip-dried
Cause not a wrinkle's found
But she never learnt to iron
Just wouldn't hang around.

If I had a choice right now
I'd choose the wrinkle-free,
And be just like my daughter
Not caring who may see.

Or I could be a nudist
And wear no clothes at all,
Although that is an option
I wouldn't have the gall.

'Cause if I passed a mirror
More wrinkles would I see,
I'd then get out the iron
So I'd be wrinkle-free.

Yes, I'll just keep on ironing
Despite my real disgust,
No matter how I hate it
I really know I MUST.

Clock Tower Secrets

I look upon your face and wonder – what secrets do you hold?
For many years you've stood in place; what stories could
    be told?
You show the time for all to see, you sweep your hands around
For those who look, there is no fee, they know where you
    are found.

Perhaps small children on their way have stopped to gaze at you
Don't know just what your big hands say, or really what you do.
Instead, they run around your base, with joyful laughter play
'Cause time for them is not a race; it's just another day.

Or could two lovers chance along, and stop to tell the time?
Their two hearts beating out one song, in melody and rhyme.
Hand in hand, their love on show, for time has now
    stopped still
With each tender kiss they know – to be in love's a thrill.

Or maybe just a businessman, who's never ever late
Will run on by – he has a plan, this time a corporate date.
To seal the deal, he must be on time, and glances once
    your way
At 1 p.m., your bell will chime, and he will have his say.

Then two old ladies pause by you, their time a precious thing
Their secrets shared, but imagine if they knew what tales of
    them you bring!
For they have stood right by your side; your face they've
    seen before
Their idle gossip you must hide, in silence must you store.

The passers-by each day they see your hands of time display
The hour and minute where they must be, on any given day.
To be correct, that is your quest – let everybody know
Reliable and at your best, you'll always be on show.

Oh yes, what stories you must hold! The tears, the love,
    the plans
Of many years could be retold, all held now in your hands.
But you will keep them safe and sound, a key will not unlock
Your silent watch that's seen and heard, all stored within
    your clock.

My Eclectic Garden

Now in my garden I will toil
fingers pottering with the soil.
I love to plant a brand-new shrub
a hole I'll dig, the roots I'll rub.
With care then put it in its place
and with my hands the dirt replace.
Yes, my garden's quite eclectic
quite descriptive and eccentric.

I love a plant with flowers bright
an instant garden's my delight.
I am not good with bulbs or seeds
they take too long to do their deeds.
But I have some, I'll have you know
and when they flower, what a show!
There are some spaces I've filled in
with Carpet of Snow – Alyssum.

In Spring, I see all tiny shoots
come through the earth, up from their roots.
Like Daffodils, in yellow bloom
and Jonquils with their sweet perfume.
But I do like a Pansy's face
in coloured rows my garden grace.
They make me smile when I walk past
because I know for months they'll last.

Carnations too are out in flood
and I can see my Roses bud.
The Daphne now has also sprung
a sweet scent wafts when Spring's begun.
Polyanthus also in the ground
with their bright colours all around.
Petunias pretty in pink and red
fill the gaps in my garden bed.

Lilac spreads with purple hue
and Violets do come up on cue.
They are all planted by my hand
to make my garden look so grand.
I see red Native Bottlebrushes
and Grevillia's gorgeous golden rushes.
May even pull a weed or two
they don't belong and spoil the view.

I'll help my plants and fertilise
to make them grow and maximise.
Through my years of random planting
I make my garden now enchanting.
So, I will potter with a smile
then in my garden sit a while.
Admire all that I have done
oh, my garden is such fun.

The Burning Torch

My darling, I am coming home, you just wait and see
I did not drown, that fateful day, into the deepest sea.
I hear you call me every night when you sit on the porch
Waiting for me to return – I see your burning torch.

It started out like any day, the sea so calm, just right
Blue cloudless skies, a gentle breeze to fill the sail so tight.
Good fishing had, 'twas time to go, we set off for homeward
    bound
We worried not about our return, thought we'd be safe
    and sound.

Clouds rolled in to blot the blue, the sea began to foam
We'd gone out miles to catch the best before we turned
    for home.
The sailors all went to their places when dark clouds began
    to form
They knew the signs were ominous, of a brewing storm.

While nets were reeled in, thunder clapped, then lightning
    sent a flare
With expert hands upon the deck, to panic would be rare.
The captain spoke, 'Now listen, men, this storm puts us to test
It seemed to come from nowhere – lads, just do your very best.'

The clouds grew dark, the waves lashed out, the ship it
    bobbed about
Lightning flashed and thunder roared, overwhelming all
    our shouts.

Our footing hard to keep on deck, all soaked from rain
    that poured
I did not see the big wave come; next we were overboard.

We thrashed about the raging sea and watched the ship
    go down
Could this be really happening? I knew that I would drown.
Though my mind was strong, my body weakened, until I
    heard your shout
'Come back to me,' but it was too late, the angry waves
    won out.

And just as I was going down, again I heard your voice
'Come back, my love, I need you here – don't leave, you have
    a choice.'
I chose to stay right by your side and be your guiding light
From where I lie on ocean's bed, I see you every night.

So yes, my love, I heard your call upon that fateful day
And though you're saddened by my loss, I have now this to say:
Do not grieve, my dearest one, please wipe away your tears
For I was with you in the past, and will stay throughout
    your years.

Now as you sit upon the porch and gaze out at the sea
Keep searching for my ship's return – one day you will see me.
I'll then smile and take your hand, and together we will go
To where life's journey does return, and only we will know.

Emergency Department

I walk from work, a smile upon my face;
a busy shift, Emergency the place.

Where sick and injured come in through the door
who we are always ready to care for.
Alarms are sounding, monitors beep,
all beds are full, and to their needs we leap.

Check vital signs, the temp, pulse, and BP
take blood, a urine test, an ECG.
Put in an IV cannula I will
if veins are difficult, it takes some skill.

Next, take them down to X-ray for a scan
or, if their bladder's full, offer a pan.
For pain, give medication, reassess
and if they vomit, I'll clean up their mess.

For patient comfort always tops the list,
and to ensure this happens, I'll assist.
When cold, a nice warm blanket brings a smile
sometimes I'll hold their hand then for a while.

With reassuring voice, allay their fears,
if they're upset then wipe away their tears.
Write up my notes on everything I've done,
hand over to the next nurse, one by one.

The hours seem to quickly run away
and soon my shift is finished for the day.
I'll say goodbye to patients in my care
be glad that on this day I have been there.

I walk from work, a smile upon my face;
a busy shift, Emergency the place.

Mother Knows Best

The phone it rang, a voice I heard
'Your son's down here, it's quite absurd.
He's with a friend, 50 each to spend!
I thought I'd ring, not message send.

Was sure that you would want to know
I'll keep them here until you show,
They've ridden down upon their bikes
That's quite a ride for little tykes.'

So the car I took on down the road
I parked outside and in I strode.
'Why hello, boys, what's that you've got?
A 50 each, that's quite a lot.

Where did you get that money, son?'
'We found it on the road, dear Mum.'
'Oh, did you now? Well fancy that
I think we need a little chat.

So come on, boys, get in my car
We'll go back home – it isn't far.
Now tell the truth about your find.'
This invitation my son declined.

Instead, he swore he found the cash
But I knew that he'd robbed my stash.
I asked again, 'The truth please tell,'
He lied once more, and I said 'Well!

I don't believe that this is so
Now to police we all must go.
'Cause little boys who tell such lies
Go straight to jail when truth is denied.'

He looked at me, his tears did swell
Ah-ha, I thought, he now will tell.
The truth from him I did coerce:
'I stole the money from your purse.'

Two frightened boys I then took home
The lesson learnt was set in stone.
'Don't lie or steal,' I told my son
'Especially not to your dear Mum.'

Disadvantaged Scholastic Parents
Pursuing Challenging Matters

The meeting's called now, ladies, we've programs to discuss
A bit of quiet's what we want, so do without the fuss.
Our children's education is the issue here today
So, listen now, I wish to speak, in a moment have your say.

We'll skip the first few pages, those now from one to three
No relevant material to us here, as you can surely see.
Now what Specific needs do our programs have to meet?
Please write it down real slowly, and try to make it neat.

Next, we have Synopsis, an educational word
Just what it means, don't ask me – it's one I've never heard.
But for publication purposes, put down now what you think
If we hurry up and pen this soon, we all can have a drink.

Evaluation Statement and Strategies achieved
Access the program's actions here, for funds you wish received.
Now, don't look so dumbfounded, an answer please do give
I didn't write the questions asked, it's the times in which
   we live.

We're getting sidetracked, ladies, your shopping lists can wait
Remember what we've come here for, and don't get so irate.
They wish to know Objectives, the Purposes, Goals and Aims
To make some sense of what they want, we really need
   our brains.

Oh dear, this is confusing, I wish I understood
I really have so much to do, go home, I wish I could.
Yet we must decide directions that our guidelines want to shape
And so to implement this plan, which practice it will take.

Goodbye now, dear, I'm glad you came – I wonder why
   she went?
I'm sure it won't be long, you'll see, to find out what
   they've meant.
For our children's sake, this load of garb we really must persist
Don't let them think we're ignorant; if in doubt, we'll make
   a list.

Our Indicators for Success, do any of you know?
I really need an answer smart, for the Minister I'll then show.
What plan we'll use, our Strategies, and how we will enforce
And don't forget to add the cost in priority of resource.

At last, I bring this meeting here to a final close
And if your head is in a spin, here's what I do propose.
Just have a laugh, a cup of tea, and let yourself unwind,
For you have been the victims of a Bureaucratic mind.

Painting Pictures

What shades of colour do we paint
while walking on this earth?
Do we leave behind a masterpiece,
or a squiggle with no worth?

Will the colours that we choose
look vibrant – do they shout?
Or are they like dull grey lead lines
so easily rubbed out?

Are all the brush strokes that you paint
precise, done with finesse?
Or are they like thick crayon scrawled
on paper in a mess?

And will you hang upon a wall
admired by the best?
Or stay unseen and never shown
remain an unfinished sketch?

The colours that you choose in life
portray your inner self.
So, are you rich, red, powerful paint
or a shade left on the shelf?

You could be bright and beautiful
in orange, yellow, green.
Or does your glossy outer fade
and quickly lose its sheen?

Are you a calm, turquoise-blue
just like a tranquil sea?
Or do you live with black or grey?
That's all you'll ever be.

The colours in my life are prime
though that can be changed
to any shade I choose to be
if mixed or rearranged.

Seek out the artist in your life
ensure he paints you true.
Be one to stand out in a crowd
there's only one of you.

My World's Eyes Are Crying

My world's eyes are crying
Big tears roll down its face,
It cries for what it sees each day
And for the human race.

My world's voice is calling
Shouts loudly every day,
It calls out, 'STOP, and listen, please,
To what I have to say.'

My world's heart is breaking
Its love has turned to hate,
So it cracks and shatters everywhere
Just what now is its fate?

My world's arms are reaching
Stretching far and wide,
It reaches out to hold man close
Embrace each one inside.

My world's legs are moving
With strides now long and fast,
It walks away so we all must
Now ponder on our past.

Please don't go away, dear world,
We need you to survive,
How can we right this awful wrong?
Please help us to revive.

And just when all is getting dark
I see a tiny light,
I think our world is turning back
To help us in our plight.

You must obey the golden rule
Bring love to everyone,
Stop all the ugly hate and war
Your one chance has begun.

Yes, dear world, I hear your words
I promise we will try,
For never do I want to see
More sad tears from your eyes.

Just Let Me Sunbake

I don't need chocolate or some wine
I don't need sex most of the time
Just let me sunbake.

No fancy house or big flash car
I don't need jewels or caviar
Just let me sunbake.

Don't need to work to buy new clothes
Or brand-new shoes… well, some of those
Just let me sunbake.

When the sun is out, I'm like a snake
Peel off my gear, no marks I'll make
Just let me sunbake.

I'll stretch out on my big beach towel
Or lie out by a swimming pool
Just let me sunbake.

To feel the warm rays on my skin
No oils or creams do I rub in
Just let me sunbake.

Please do not tell me 'Don't do that!'
Or give advice to slip, slop, slap
Just let me sunbake.

When sun shines down you'll hear me shout
I'll find a place and stretch right out
Just let me sunbake.

Doesn't take much to make me happy
I have good friends and family
They let me sunbake.

And when the sun sets in the sky
I'll wait until I see it rise
Just let me sunbake.

The Day When Christmas Burned

There was movement all across our land, as candles
   burned so bright
With carols sung and stockings hung on Christmas Eve,
But little did we all suspect upon this sacred night,
That lightning then would strike with no reprieve.
A single bolt hit the ground and lit the undergrowth,
In bushlands tinder-dry ready to burn,
Fire would release its fury – to wreak havoc was its oath,
The aftermath of disaster we'd soon learn.

It started out along the coast, in a little seaside town
A lovely spot to soak up all the sun,
Where tourists came from near and far, many had come down
But soon we'd see them on the run.
The fire sirens soon rang out, they warned impending doom:
Leave your homes, this fire's out of control,
Forget your earthly souvenirs, for them you have no room,
Just save yourselves; do not become its toll.

The fire licked and danced about, its hot breath could not
    be quenched,
It raced along the hills of coastal scene,
Destroying all within its path, with water could not
    be drenched,
The blackened earth would show where it had been.
Red-hot embers flew about, crisscrossed above the trees,
And sparks they crackled as they did ignite,
This mighty hound brought houses down, fanned by a hot
    north breeze
Hell had no justice on that dreadful night.

It would not let up, its smoke grew thick, the fire raced
    through the town
And down the ocean road it had its way,
It melted cars, strong winds prevailed, its flames would not
    back down,
Would be foolhardy if you chose to stay.
Evacuate, get children out, these cries were heard for miles
Time was now against these weary folk,
But safety was within their reach – they managed to survive,
Their faces black, with teary eyes they spoke.

The heat was more than man could stand; it forced them
    to retreat
But they came back with strength they'd found next day,
'We'll take you on, you mangy beast, for we will not be beat!'
And so, on bended knees began to pray.
The firefighters did their best, brave efforts we revere
For not one human life was lost that night,
But birds and wildlife suffered much when this monster
    did appear,
It took their lives with fast and furious might.

Blackened hillsides do remain, silhouettes on turquoise surf
Like skeletons against the sea so blue,
The children's toys all black and scorched are strewn upon
    the earth,
No houses left for Santa to come to.
And memories of a lifetime gone, how quickly the fire erased
Its wrath no mercy did restrain,
But they'll rebuild; new strength they'll find, their challenges
    will face,
And Christmas carols will be sung again.

Our Grains Of Sand

Our sands of time we do receive
upon our days of birth.
Just what we do with them each day
is the measure of our worth.

Some build great castles high and grand
adorned with finest jewels.
While others let sand drift away
and live their lives as fools.

But just one grain kept really safe
and treasured through one's life,
can make a difference every day
and keep us out of strife.

Some sands are course and rough to hold
and some are fine and pure.
How we treat our grains of sand
shapes what we'll get for sure.

When I look back upon my sand
I've kept it pretty well
shared it around and reaped rewards
my grains I'd never sell.

My sand is mixed with others' too
my friends and family's
who share the beach I lie upon
their sands so close to me.

And on the day my grains run out
and I am buried deep
I'll give them all just one last speck
of my sand to keep.

So, hold your sands and treasure them
take care of every grain
and you will reap the benefits
you have so much to gain.

High Society

Now I have been to many dos that put me to the test,
Where I have drank beer and wine, sipped champagne with
   the best.
But this weekend I'll now recall, right here in Melbourne town,
It takes the cake as functions go, an experience to put down.

We all arrived, the motel booked two months or more ahead,
To our surprise a double meant you shared two single beds.
'Worry not,' Fiona said, she knows what she's about
'Just come with me to the front desk, I'll have this sorted out.'

A feed of Chinese, what a treat, before a taxi call,
For an evening with the footy crew at the Moonee Ponds
   Town Hall.
With suitcases open, we donned our garb, although the theme
   was school
We dressed up in our finery, so not to look the fool.

Then stamped and issued with a glass, we stood around to chat,
When Mother's legs got tired, she sat down at the back.
But little did she think she'd see a show she'd not forget!
With the crowd in gathered circles, we had the stage now set.

Some folks were in a happy mood, let's party! was the go,
And to the back this blonde now went, the crowd she had
   to show –
Lifting up her tunic high, she flashed the boys her bum.
Them her tattooed rear impressed, but really shocked my mum.

In the main hall where the music was, we had a feed of beef,
No tables free, on the floor we sat, with plates upon our knees.
And then to dance, the music loud, a disco atmosphere
But Mum and Dad, this noise to stop, put a serviette in each ear.

Now Dad was getting anxious too, for his poem he longed
   to read,
The DJ got him up on stage, we hoped he would succeed.
But the crowd was not receptive, let fly with stale old buns
So better luck next time, Dad, you can't compete with bums.

Then Greg thought he would fix it up, get Billy over here,
To meet our dad and make things right, create a little cheer.
But somewhere on the way Greg found a Duckworth hard
   to shove
And we all thought a fight was on when the push got
   rather rough.

However, good things come to pass, this evening drew to a close,
We ventured back for a cup of tea, for some a little doze.
For others, their stomach did not hold, the bowl became
    a friend
As you can see, our big night out came to a fitting end.

So, if you want excitement, lads – good cheer, strip shows,
    and fights –
It's all down there in Melbourne, at the Essendon footy nights.
I'm sure the Dons would welcome you, and now when all
    is said
I'll charge my glass, raise my hand, and salute the black and red.

I'd

The time has passed so quickly, regrets I have a few,
I'd change some aspects of my life, and some I'd start anew.
I'd go out in the rain to walk, no umbrella overhead,
Arms outstretched, I'd let the rain soak me through instead.

I'd smile and say hello to strangers on the street
Instead of staring straight ahead it could be you I'd greet.
And if I passed a flower bed, I'd stop to smell the rose,
And let its lovely perfume waft right up my nose.

I'd let the dog free from the lead, no doo would I pick up,
And throw the ball far the air, yelling: 'Go fetch it, pup!'
I'd sing out loud without a care, whatever I sounded like,
In karaoke bars line up and overtake the mike.

I'd sing Baa, Baa, Black Sheep, not rainbow red or blue,
Read Noddy to the children, Mr. Plod and Big Ears too.
I'd dress up just like Santa, and call out 'Ho, ho, ho!'
Pinch Xmas trees from the bush, sing carols that I know.

I'd slurp my drink and chew my food, my mouth kept
    open wide,
So, if you don't approve of that, then please don't sit beside.
At the movies I would rattle bags – no, I don't think I'd do that
There are some things I would not change no matter
    where I'm at.

I wouldn't sweep the floor sometimes, nor would I make
   the bed,
But laze around just reading books and watching TV instead.
I'd wear my clothes unironed, wouldn't polish up my shoes,
Eat several blocks of chocolate and never watch the news.

Place my elbow on the table, put my feet up on the couch,
And if you said do take them off, I'd say 'Don't be a grouch!'
I'd scratch the soup bowl with my spoon, from the knife lick
   butter off,
And if I had a tickly throat, uncovered I would cough.

I'd wear short skirts at 60, high heels that make a noise,
Forget the men with greying hair – I'd ogle all the boys.
I'd turn the music up real loud, and drown the neighbours out,
Instead of being nice and quiet I'd often scream and shout.

I'd pierce my nose and get some tatts, and show them off
   with style,
I'd let my hair go really grey and wear a toothless smile.
I'd hang out with a bikie gang, now wouldn't that be fun?
But I would run and hide away if they brought out a gun.

I'd say what I was thinking, I wouldn't hold things back,
This 'Political Correctness' now is all a load of crap.
We're told to watch our Ps and Qs; well, I have had enough
And if I offend you with my words, I couldn't give a stuff.

I'd let the grandkids make a mess, and wouldn't bat an eye
I'd welcome them with open arms, not whinge or growl or cry.
And every time they came to stay, we'd stay up late at night
To watch the scary movies and squeal or howl in fright.

You see, the years go quickly by; it's not long before you're old.
What is the mark that you have left, or stories that you've told?
So, if you have a bucket list, now do them one by one,
Don't worry what the others think – go out and have more fun!

My Just-In-Case Case

Now, when I go on holiday, I'm never sure what I will pack,
'cause once I am then on the road there is no turning back.

So, I begin with good intent, I'll sort and pile my clothes
then I'll decide just what to take – my shoes, I must pack those.

But wait, I'll look, that shirt I'll need, some jumpers to
  keep warm,
I'd better take those brand-new shoes that I have never worn.

Can't forget my underwear and swimming costumes too
bikinis, two or three of them – selections, need a few.

Some formal clothes I must include, high heels and a nice dress
'cause going out for dinner needs attire to impress.

Oh, deary me, I can't decide just what to leave behind
For if I leave it out, I know I'll find I'm in a bind.

My case is tight, the zips near bust, but I just push more in,
my pulse it rises with great fear – I cannot leave one thing!

So then I think, Oh, please don't fret, I have a good idea
I'll just pack myself another case to take my extra gear.

Yes, that is how it came about, I knew just what to do,
for all the choices I may have I'll always carry two.

One, for all essential things that I cannot replace,
the others full of maybe-needs, My Just-In-Case Case.

An Artist's Brush

The artist's brush creates his scene
with brush strokes, drips, and dabs,
upon the canvas bringing life
his palette's colours bright.

The sky of grey suggests the rain
mist is silver shimmering sheen,
blots of pink, green, gold, and blue,
white lines distinguish path and road.

Tall buildings drawn as earthy stone
their spires rising to the sky.
Dark stripes denote the windowpanes
rooftops in red and yellow shades.

Brown branches stroked with green
create the tree-lined promenade,
white streaks imprint the vehicles' wheels
marks left while driving in the rain.

Streetlights shine bright, the clock nears three
imagery brings life to canvas blank,
an era now no longer seen,
where folks, unhurried, go about their day.

These images mere lines and strokes
painted by an artist's skilful hands,
created with colour, depth and warmth
although a rainy day, invite a walk.

I'm Glad You Are My Mother

I'm glad you are my mother
for this I have no doubt,
you've given me good values
I've used in life throughout.
You're always there to hold me
and soothe away my pain,
you lift me up if I am down
and set me straight again.
I would be lost without you
though try I cannot find
the words to ever thank you enough,
I know you will not mind.

But there is still another
who must be mentioned now,
for guidance and good wisdom
he's always right somehow.
And that would be my father
a man I do admire
his words and kindness given free
these traits I do aspire.
I often read his poetry
his words are written down,
I'll never be as good as him
but thank him anyhow.

And still, I have some more to thank
my sisters and my brothers,
who shared my life when we were kids
still do; they're like no others.
We often get together now
and laugh about our past,
tell jokes and stories of good times
shared memories always last.
And to my in-law family
they've given me so much
I get along with everyone
and love the entire bunch.

But now I really must expand
to include my friends as well,
I couldn't live without their love
as each one I often tell.
Cross paths with them when least expected
but then we'll take the time
to bring each other up to date
I'm glad that they are mine.
We laugh and share the good and bad
hug each other when we meet,
from many different worlds they come
they make my life complete.

Yet best of all I'll save to last
without them I wouldn't be:
my darling husband, he's my rock;
my great kids, there are three.
I treasure all the memories
so many we have made,
they fill my life with love each day
not one would I ever trade.
I'll not forget my in-laws' kids
each one I do adore,
It's time to tell them how I feel
they're great – of this, I'm sure.

Grandkids six complete this tale
each one a special child,
I watch them grow and see their love
they all have me beguiled.
We must have others in our lives
to share our journey with
appreciate them one by one
there's so much that they give.
So, take the time to tell them all
how much they mean to you,
before it's too late and you have gone;
for this, you can't undo.

Does My Bum Look Big In This?

Today I saw two great big bums
Both packed in real tight shorts,
Tried not to stare, but then this pair
Were not good-lookin' sorts.

Their bottoms wobbled all around
While they were walkin' by,
Could only see in front of me
They caught my very eye.

I wondered if these ladies knew
How big were their behinds,
Encased real tight, both were a sight
They didn't seem to mind.

I worked real hard to stop my grin
And tried to look elsewhere,
But as they walked, some others gawked
You couldn't help but stare.

I then rushed home and backed my butt
In front of mirrored glass,
Maybe it's me, but I couldn't see
Any issues with my arse.

After frantic search, my husband I found
He said, 'What's up, dear Chris?'
'Look at me here, check out my rear
Does my bum look big in this?'

My husband frowned, looked up and down
As he sized up my rear,
His answer he knew, his smile it grew
'Your bum looks fine, my dear.'

He Watched With Love

He watched with love, eyes filled with pride
Walked slowly down the aisle his bride.
Down slowly walked the aisle his bride
He watched with love, eyes filled with pride.

To him she walked with style and grace
Tears freely poured on down his face.
Poured freely tears on down his face
To him she walked with style and grace.

With hand in hand they soon were wed
Vows both declared with love when said.
Declared both vows with love when said
With hand in hand they soon were wed.

He watched with love, eyes filled with pride
Walked slowly down the aisle his bride.
To him she walked with style and grace
Tears freely poured on down his face.
With hand in hand they soon were wed
Vows both declared with love when said.

Good Intentions

This story's one I'd like to tell
Of when disaster struck.
And how all my good intentions
Turned quickly into muck.
It happened on one Friday eve
I was the fill-in chef,
I thought I'd cook a real nice treat
It ended up a mess.

A salmon can I opened first
Chopped onion for some flavour,
I thought some creamed corn would be fine
Mashed potato one would savour.
A patty was my aim to make
But this mixture was rather thin,
So, a bit of flour and one Weet-Bix
To thicken it next went in.

I placed these patties in the pan
And hoped they wouldn't burn,
But things got worse, no matter how
I tried, they would not turn.
And seated round the table were
My father, daughter, and cousin Brent
All hungry, waiting patiently
A hard day's work they'd spent.

So finally, I served them up
But the truth I think I knew,
When Father, he just raised his eyes
And said they were like glue.
But there was one, my friend indeed
Who didn't seem to mind,
He ate them all, the taste he liked
Old Drum, the shaggy kind.

Then, again I came this week
To be once more the cook,
But you can be sure this time I brought
My trusted cookery book.
My family has to be content
With a chop or perhaps a snag,
For never again would I cook that fish
For it to end up clag.

So, to all you fishermen on the bay
I offer up this prayer:
Bring me a cod, a flake or bream
Just leave the salmon there.

Civic Hall Lament

There is movement at the council
for the word is quite financial:
the funds for Civic Hall have now run dry.
They had set aside eight million
but have wasted over a squillion,
and wonder why the public surely cry.

So, just what have you been doing?
'Cause it looks like we're in ruin
I can't believe where all the money went –
just getting some opinions
and consultants by the billions
yet still no blasted plans for what's been spent.

I will ask you now some questions
and maybe make some more suggestions.
Perhaps you'd better burn it to the ground
then collect all its insurance
but give us some assurance
You'll keep it in the coffers safe and sound.

And amongst the ashes build us
a big shrine made of bulldust
'cause that is what you feed us every day.
No wonder we are cynical
your promises just mythical,
we can't believe a blasted word you say.

We don't need a 'market process'
to extract us from this mess,
or feasibility studies by the score.
Or fancy words to blind us –
we're sick of all that you discuss,
just get the blasted job done, we implore.

But I'll bet there's no reaction
with this council's lack of action,
or excuses for their wasteful overspend.
So, I will keep informing you
be sure that you would want me to
and hope quite soon this saga here may end.

Cinderella's 'Ugly Sister'

A pantomime I've been in
'Twas Cinderella once again.
But not the Cinders role, you see
Instead, an 'Ugly Sister' – ME.

And with my other sister mean
Made Cinderella sweep and clean.
You see, this role before I've played
My first time ever upon the stage.

I was just twelve, now 65
This Ugly Sister role revived.
We made the children laugh and shout
Cause Ugly Sisters mucked about.

But Fairy Godmother, she got mad,
And punished us when we were bad.
Her magic wand had us entranced
She tucked our dresses into our pants.

When the kids, seeing our knickers,
Called out loud, the parents snickered.
Then at the ball we danced around
And even the poor prince he frowned.

We tried to win the prince's heart
But Cinderella did us outsmart!
So, we two sisters felt unloved
Into the cupboard, Cinders shoved.

'Cause when the prince came with the shoe
We tried to make it fit us too.
Then he asked, 'Are there any more?'
The kids all screamed, 'Behind that door!'

Upon Cinders this slipper was tried,
The Ugly Sisters' plan backfired.
And so, of course, you know the rest
A happy ending was the best.

The audience they clapped and cheered
For our final bows we each appeared.
My kids and grandies came to see
They thought I made a good 'Ugly'.

And for next year I do await,
For pantomimes are really great.
They keep me young, I have a ball
My age deters me NOT at all.

Mum's Favourites

I have three favourite children – how lucky can I be?
I need to tell each one of them how much they mean to me.
For I am blessed each day, I know, they think of me with love,
No greater gift I shall ever want, I thank you all above.

To my favourite daughter dear, your beauty shines so bright,
Your loving heart and thoughtful ways will always be your light.
At times, I see a bit of me in what you say or do,
And smile in quiet secrecy because I'm that part of you.

I've watched you grow into who you are, no prouder Mum
   than I,
My heart is filled with love for you no wealth could ever buy.
And when we stroll down memory lane, or share the good
   and bad,
I hope you'll smile and think of times together we have shared.

And so, dear girl, this truth I say – you are my favourite one,
As daughters go, you are the best; I'm glad that I'm your mum.
And I will always treasure this, our bond so true and strong,
For where you go, I'll always be, beside you right along.

Now to my favourite firstborn son, I have so much to say,
I look at you and burst with pride, especially on this day.
Your will is strong, just like mine, I gave you this for free,
And every time you use it so, you'll feel the love from me.

I see into your heart and find a true and loyal friend,
A strong determined mind you have, these strengths you
    truly blend.
You make me laugh, you're not afraid to show just who you are,
Don't ever change your inner self, for this will take you far.

I hope you know what joy you bring as a favourite son of mine,
I'll always hold you dear to me, I'm glad that you are mine.
And through the path you choose to go, I will be by your side,
Be not afraid to take a leap, explore the far and wide.

And next, my favourite second boy – my son, I've watched
    you grow
Into a loving gentle man, such kindness you do show.
A quiet nature deep and true, a calmness you possess,
And yet at your endless funny ways my laughter can't
    be suppressed.

You work so hard in all you do, take pride in what you make,
Don't ask for much, just some respect, give more than you
   do take.
A country boy you are at heart, this part you got from me,
So never lose it and wisely use it to shape your destiny.

How proud I am to call you son, a favourite like no other,
I could not ask for any more when you do call me Mother.
I'll always answer you and smile at our every meeting
And kiss your cheek and hug you tight, for this will be
   my greeting.

And so, my favourite children three, this rhyme I now do end,
And hope that when you read my words, you'll see the love
   I send.
For me there are no other ones I'd ever want to choose,
You are my shining lights of joy I never want to lose.

My Cardboard Cut-Out Husband Returns

My husband has gone fishing with his mates,
a week without him here would be so great.
But now I'm all alone, left here on my own,
for his return I'll sit around and wait.

But no, by Jove, I have another plan,
my cardboard cut-out is my other man.
My mind is in a spin, I'll go rescue him,
dress him up and make him spick and span.

He's been folded for a while, so it may take some time
to bring him back to life and make him mine.
I bring him out to play when my real one goes away,
my cardboard cut-out husband is divine.

We will sit and watch shows on our TV,
he won't argue with the ones I want to see.
No meals I will prepare, he really doesn't care,
he is the perfect husband now for me.

In case you are in wonder, you I will remind,
I really haven't gone and lost my mind.
It was really for a joke when I made this cardboard bloke,
for a special date, my husband I couldn't find.

He was hard at work in another state,
and could not come home to be my dinner date.
So for a little fun, I created a new one,
to bring out at any time to be my mate.

When my man does return, I'll fold this one away,
my cardboard cut-out stored for another day.
But I'll keep him just in case my husband I must replace,
For times when he is gone, this closet one will stay.

Looking Glass

As I gaze into the mirror, whose reflection do I see?
A face with lines and greying hair, how could that now be me?
Where is the pretty little girl with cheeks of rosy red?
And big brown eyes and ringlet curls, with bows tied on
    her head?

I see her face of innocence, her childish laughter's gay
I see her running wildly round, her squeals in fun and play.
Yearning for her fresh, sweet face, the sparkle in her eyes
Instead, I see deep tired lines – this mirror tells no lies.

I look again and there she is, this time a bit more grown
This teenage girl with hair now bobbed and style that is
    her own.
Years move on, a woman now, with youth still on her face
With long dark hair and ruby lips, elegance and grace.

Each day the mirror tells its tale, the years have quickly passed
Although I try, I cannot stop my youth from fading fast.
Some days, looking into this glass, I hardly recognise
That woman with a saggy jaw, and crow's feet round her eyes.

I wonder when the time will come that the girl I will not see
And only in my mind will I still know that she is me.
For there's one thing that is certain: we cannot stop our age
Each day our lives are written down, and our face is just a page.

Sue's Journey

My sister Sue had a mammogram recall, so went with
   trepidation
Then I received her miserable call, and to her side did hasten.
Wet tears flowed down her cheek, 'A breast lump they
   have found
'Twas hard to find, but when they scanned, it showed
   on ultrasound.'

A biopsy next they did perform, she dreaded diagnosis
Some cells have gone and now reformed, what would be
   her prognosis?
'I'm sorry, Sue, you have CA, metastases in your breast.'
These words I heard her GP say left us both distressed.

We went with sadness in our hearts to tell our dear old mum
Her tears welled up and soon were spent, to a mother's dread
   succumbed.
But Sue was strong and wouldn't break, 'Be dammed if I'll let
   it win!'
And as she set about defeating it, she wore a steely grin.

And so, her journey then began, with appointments every day
The doctors all had made a plan to rid her of CA.
To the oncology ward she went, let chemo take a hold
To shrink this tumour was the aim – it worked, we all
   were told.

But there were costs: her hair fell out, so she went to buy a wig
She wore it well, without a doubt, and no-one did ever twig.
Her body was in a ravaged state, but her will remained
   real strong
There were more trials she had to face, and with her I
   went along.

Next came the knife, her breast removed, mastectomy complete
The surgeon's skills to us were proved, no other could compete.
More chemo then for my dear Sue, to mop up cells still there
Then rounds of radiation, almost too much to bear.

It's been a long and daunting road, with uncertainty lined
But strength and courage Sue did show with every step s
   he climbed.
She went through all the treatment well, combatted all the fear
But really, only time will tell if she stays in the clear.

Next on the list, a breast recon, then prosthesis she won't need
'Twill make up for what cancer robbed, whole again indeed!
I look at her with glowing pride; despite all she's been through
Each step she conquered in her stride, my lovely sister Sue.

Yes, now Sue's joined up with the rink, a bona fide subscriber
She wears with pride the colour pink, a cancer-free survivor.
And so, dear Lord, now hear my prayer: please keep her
   safe and sound
My sister is so dear to me. Let no more lumps be found.

Local Snakes

Local snakes! the sign did say, as I walked my dogs
So, I kept my eyes peeled out for any moving logs.
I don't like snakes – they give me the creeps,
Avoid them at all cost,
So briskly did I walk along, no time would now be lost.

I scanned the bush and undergrowth, my eyes did dart around
A little nervous if I saw some movement on the ground.
I reined the dogs in tightly,
They never went ahead,
'Cause I don't trust their wanderings; they can stay with
    me instead.

We have a wide array of snakes, some fast with good eyesight
Just lurking on my path at times, they give me such a fright.
Eastern browns and tiger snakes,
These ones quite common here,
If seen, I'll stop to let them pass and still my rising fear.

What was that now? One dog had stopped, and peered out at
    the scrub
My heart sped up and palms did sweat – was something near
    that shrub?
But then I saw it slowly move,
Quick breath I did intake,
It's only an echidna, boys, and not a bloody snake!

Silent Wonder

As I sit here now to ponder, I really start to wonder
Just what the world would be without a sound.
No noises to distract me, instead I'd find it could be
A quiet silence noticed all around.

No sound of children's laughter when each other they'd
   run after
Bringing squeals with such delight when they are caught.
Not to hear their happy chatter on subjects that to them matter
But silent conversation that means naught.

Never hearing one word, 'Mum', from the lips of my dear son
Would be something I really couldn't bear.
Not to hear when my child sings, and the joy to me that brings
Instead, I'd stand in silence and just stare.

Nor the tweeting of a bird – this sound be never heard
As it sits and chirps quite early in the morn.
Or the rooster as it crows, just because it really knows
It's time to break night's silence with each dawn.

Or the patter of the rain upon rooftops once again
Loud thunder then the lightning in a storm.
Not to hear the big waves smash upon the rocks as they
   do crash
Without this sound could only watch them form.

Never hearing music play sweet melodies through the day
Or listen to the dialogue from my shows.
Nor hear some conversation while waiting at a station
And miss the train's long whistle when it blows.

I would surely feel alone without my telephone
No ring to make me run and take a call.
Just in time I would retrieve it, pick it up and then receive it
A friendly voice would disturb me not at all.

So, I won't be beholden or say silence is so golden
I'd rather have this noisy world around.
Thank the Lord now for my hearing, all those sounds that
   are endearing
I hope I never know life without sound.

All In

There was movement out at Mollongghip, for word had
    passed around
that the 'All In' poetry slam was on the way.
'Contestants now, we need them,' all the organisers said
'I hope we get a few out for this day.'
All the tried and noted writers were convinced that they
    could win
so began to put their thoughts upon a page.
Because to be the best this day, their poems must stand out
when they recite them up on centre stage.

There was Paterson, now he could write a damn good
    Aussie yarn
he'd do one 'bout a Snowy River ride.
A story of hard-riding men and one who'd save the day
when racing down a dangerous mountainside.
Yes, that would be the winning one; he'd surely take the prize
this poem would be famous like the rest.
He'd mention his mate Clancy, from the Overflow, of course,
but the 'Man from Snowy River' was the best.

Next, Dorothea Mackellar thought she too would have a go
compose a rhyme about our Aussie land.
A weather forecast she'd include of droughts and flooding rains
or perhaps on climate change she'd take a stand.
Discuss this great big country all bathed in green and gold
the mountain ranges, jewelled seas as well,
Ah yes, she thought, that'll do it, by Jove, I'll have them beat
it really will be quite an easy sell.

But neither had considered that there might be someone else
who'd come along and sweep them both away.
By writing a great sonnet or a haiku just for fun
compose a funny limerick to say.
Yes, to be all in this contest, one must be quite versatile
and ready with selections to read out.
But it really does not matter if you win, lose, or draw
Just being here is what All In's about.

Airport Wait

At the airport, waiting for my plane, I looked around and saw
Heads all down, screens alight, conversation naught.
People sitting, concentrating, fingers flying fast,
No discussion, silently watching, no hello or goodbye.
Laptops open, apps displaying, checking data shown
Chips are crunching, gum is popping, eyes all cast down,
Earphones hanging, noiselessly watching, I secretly smile.
Silent sitting, people staring, no expression shown.
Books are open, pages turning, another chapter gone,
I am writing, quietly observing, time is ticking by.
Arms are crossing, legs are stretching, others pacing around,
Some stay seated, many standing, lined up for the call.
Delay in boarding, steward calling, apologies announced.
People wriggling, children whining, boredom rising fast,
Glitch in system, technology failing, repairs still underway.
Time's a-ticking, people sighing, hoping not too long,
Boarding happening, bags we're gathering, priority
   passengers called.
Gates have opened, people moving, stewards checking passes,
Seats now filling, belts all fastening, purring engine heard.
People chatting, lights are shining, doors are all closed,
Announcement broadcast, safety demo, wheels rolling down.
Captain speaking, welcome given, lift off happening,
   too late now,
Sit relaxing; we are flying, finally homeward bound.

A Haunting Tale

The house is haunted, so they say
for many years I have walked past.
But I went in the other day
with stumbling steps that were quite fast.

On this morning, as I drew near
I fought my way through all the grass.
No more this house would hold my fear
pushed it aside so I could pass.

Up to the door my breath I held
this new adventure had begun.
My rising fear inside I quelled,
but thought it was too late to run.

I knocked and waited patiently
though really wished then I could go.
The door it opened silently
I swallowed hard and said, 'Hello.'

A woman dressed in finery
said, 'Hello, Rose, do come inside.'
Held out her hand to welcome me
I went, although quite petrified.

But she just said, 'Come in, my dear
our visitors to us are few.
Be not afraid, there's naught to fear
we all have been expecting you.'

So once inside, I looked around
at chandeliers and carpet grand.
Surprised at what I really found
the décor lovely, so well-planned.

While all outside was in neglect
Inside it was a pleasant find.
'Twas nothing like I did suspect.
the woman also seemed so kind.

'Dear Rose, please sit, this is your place
do tell us now without delay!'
A smile appeared upon her face.
'What brought you here to us today?

Some rumours, no doubt, you have heard,
like all who pass through our front door,'
she said, while tea was being poured,
'they can't go back to life before.

But those outside have been misled
do not believe those silly lies.
They say we are the living dead,
yet as you see, we're quite alive.

Now, drink the tea we've made for you.'
I sipped; the flavour was divine.
For visitors, this special brew
sent tingles up and down my spine.

As cake was served upon my plate
I thanked them for a lovely day.
To be polite, I quickly ate
then said, 'I must be on my way.'

I turned and bid them all farewell,
and hurried home – my kids were there.
I rushed inside, so much to tell
but as I spoke, I saw them stare.

I heard them say, 'Was that someone?'
Their faces blank, they did not see.
They looked around. 'Is that you, Mum?'
I tried to tell them, 'Yes, it's me.'

Then realised – I WAS DEAD!
and felt an awful panic rise.
Those rumours were true! I had been led
naively to my own demise.

I raised my voice and tried to shout
again, this time, let out a scream.
They did not hear, for naught came out
Then I awoke – 'twas all a dream.

A Perfect Family Storm

A perfect storm is brewing against my family seas
Calm waters are now tossing to and fro.
It started with a rumble, as clouds formed overhead
Not sure from which direction it will blow.

Strong waves roll, lash the shore, wetting all the sand
I dare not dip my toe into the sea.
The undercurrent's grip is strong, weakening my stand
From both sides now I feel the pull on me.

I fear a lightning strike is near, its flash a telling sign
Hear rumbling of the thunder overhead.
The clouds are black, bearing heavy rain,
Threatening signs that fill my soul with dread.

My tears like rain freely run, streaming down my face
My heartfelt sobs keep rising in my chest.
The elements beyond control, this time may not abate
I know I must stand strong to pass this test.

Past storms have come and gone away, seas returned to calm
Bright sunny skies brought warmth upon the ground.
Yet this hurricane that's forming now, its tide is rising fast
If waves stay deep, could then my future drown?

I cannot stop the surging swell, the breakers rushing in
Against the rocks I feel my body thrown.
The fury of lashing waves, whipping at my soul
Could they forever change the peace I've known?

Sometimes the outcome of a storm is subject to its force
Destructive winds may tear apart your home.
A rebuild then the only way to make foundations strong
Replacing shifting sands this time with stone.

Reel Him In

With broken romances, take more chances
There's plenty of fish in the sea.
To find a good dish, you must learn how to fish
And what a good catch he will be.

Your rod must be long and the line very strong
When you cast it's all in the swing.
First bait up your hook, so he'll take a good look
And never be frightened to fling.

Raise your arm high, and let your line fly
Entice with a big juicy worm.
Then with a big grin, you'll reel him in
And watch him wriggle and squirm.

If he's short on good measure or gives you no pleasure
Just throw him right back to the sea.
Then bait up again because you don't know when
The next one you catch may agree.

You'll know with one look that he's taken the hook
While you reel him in, he won't fight.
When he's on dry land, and you brush off the sand
His scales will be shiny and bright.

Beware of the shark, which will hide in the dark
To appear when you least expect.
Keep your eye out, and if ever in doubt
Be quick, cut the line, and reject.

Fishing is fun when you snag the right one
That becomes the catch of the day.
You will be satisfied, whether grilled or deep-fried
When you cook, he won't have a say.

From The Other Side

Do not weep for me, my love,
my time was up; I had to leave.
Received the calling from above
I watch as you now sadly grieve.

Your heart is broken, so is mine
my tears cascade like falling rain.
My destiny to walk the line
in death, I too can feel your pain.

You must go on without me there,
and when you think of me, know this.
The love we had was ours to share
each other bound in wedded bliss.

My time on earth is up, it's true,
I've crossed now to the other side.
I ask, my darling, this from you:
forgive the fact that I have died.

I had to leave, I had no choice,
although I'm gone, you'll feel me near.
Close your eyes, and hear my voice
call out to you, 'I love you, dear.'

But you still have so much to do,
I'll wait until you come to me.
And when your time is also through
together, then, we'll always be.

Winter Ecstasy

My icy fingers on your skin
At last I'm here, so let's begin
To take the warmth now from your soul
And cool it down with Winter's toll.

Send tingles up your lovely spine
What pleasures given will be divine
I'll strip you bare to lie with me
And feel your inner ecstasy.

I'll curl your toes with freezing sin
And make you want me deep within
You'll beg for more, I'll feel your thrill
Your racing heart will never still.

To see you melt beneath my touch
For me will almost be too much
I'll take my time to make you cold
Ensure you'll shiver from my hold.

And when you've reached your climax high
I'll know you are entirely mine
You'll never want a warming bed
When you can have my touch instead.

Just before the Spring appears
I'll leave your side, but have no fear
For I'll return one Winter night
Reclaim your soul and hold you tight.

I Have To Feed Alfred

I have a dear friend, her mind's gone away,
No longer remembers the time of the day.
The dread and the anguish I see in her eyes
She asks, 'Why am I here?' We tell her white lies.

'I want to go home, please open the door,
I've got to feed Alfred, my cat I adore.
I'll just get my bag, then to the street I'll go
To buy him more food, he'll be hungry, you know.

Oh, I want to leave, but the door's always locked.'
She looks straight at me; 'But your name I've forgot.
I don't understand what exactly I've done.
And why I'm kept here – please tell me, dear one?'

Her memory loss started a few years ago
At first, it was small things that she didn't know.
Then over the last year had a rapid decline.
Became befuddled – an ominous sign.

Still driving her car, she would park in the street
But then she'd forget where we were to meet.
So, we'd give her a ring to guide her our way
And when she arrived, 'Silly me!' she would say.

It got to the stage where she no longer drove,
At home was a danger with things on the stove.
Her health soon went downhill, her memory lost
In care she's been placed; but oh, what the cost.

Jean's mind is still active, she can't understand
Why she must stay here, it's not what she planned.
She begs and she pleads, 'Can't you see where I'm at?
I must go home to feed Alfred, my cat.'

And so, I must leave her, my eyes filled with tears
I think of the good times we've shared through the years.
Although her mind's left her, dementia has won,
We'll still come to visit, for she's our dear one.

Not Going Anywhere

I have been really busy, I babysat all day
My grandkids four, all girls, you see, came over for a play.
We went into the Tangled Maze, got lost and just had fun,
Played mini golf and laser force, ice skated on the run.

Then back we came to draw and paint, played a board game
    one or two
They never stopped smiling all day, we had so much to do.
I love the kids to come around, they fill my heart with joy,
I spoil them all with lots of love and buy them brand new toys.

And when they had to go back home, I kissed them all goodbye
'Do come again, and make it soon!' 'We will,' was their reply.
The house was a mess, but I cleaned it up with a smile upon
    my face,
I'm glad they like to be with me, their love I can't replace.

And so that night when I lay down to rest my weary head
I didn't think my time was up – next morn, I woke up dead!
'Dead,' they said, 'how can that be? I wonder what went
    wrong?'
I saw them all with teary cheeks. 'Hey, wait, I won't be long!

I am not dead, it's just a dream, this nightmare must now stop
Don't take me, please, I will not go, don't give to me the
    chop.'
They gathered round to take a look, my lifeless body still
But I'm not going anywhere, death's just not in my will.

When I saw their crying eyes, my heart it gave a thump
My little girls will save me now – come on, my heart, just
    pump.
I worked real hard to them return, and then I took a breath
'A miracle!' they all called out, the day I cheated death.

'Oh, Nan, you're back with us again, we knew you would not
    leave!'
'What's all this fuss you talk about? You're far too young to
    grieve.'
And that is how my day turned out, for such a tangled maze
To wake up dead, that's not for me – it's all now just a haze.

Do You Remember, Jim?

I can't believe you're 60, Jim, those years now in our past,
Still, memories made will never fade, but last.
I remember when – we were kids back then – out on the farm
    with Dad,
Both young and free, a lot to see, and so much fun we had.

Our collie dog, his name was Bob, we loved to play with him,
His coat was lush, we'd pat and brush. Do you remember, Jim?
It must be said, up in the shed, that old green door we'd read,
Those words all pencilled, sketches stencilled, history now
    indeed.

And how we fed those poddy calves and pigs all in their sty,
I recollect the eggs we'd get, then make the chickens fly.
The mushies out, we'd scream and shout, and run fast down
    the hill,
To pick the lot, for Nana's pot, so we could eat our fill.

And in the spring at harvest time, we'd watch as Dad baled hay,
That green band tight, those bales took flight, he'd stack them
    up all day.
Then back we'd go, 'cause we would know our Nan would
    have a spread,
A good cook she! We'd have our tea, before we went to bed.

At times upon our grandpa's knee, we'd sit while he did sing
The songs he'd know, like Old Black Joe, forgetting not a thing.
And if unruly, he would surely flick the razor strop,
Reminding us, 'Be good, you two, your nonsense please
    do stop.'

To Dead Horse Corner, up a tree, that sticky gum we'd pull,
But never went where we weren't meant – the paddock with
    the bull.
When blackies grew, we picked a few, our billies overflowed.
Then juicy pie for you and I, our bellies overloaded.

The visitors, they came and went, our family, friends we had,
But one named Ray just couldn't say, his words he stuttered bad.
I remember we would grin with glee, while hiding out of sight,
We laughed at him – yes, guilty, Jim – not sorry for his plight.

We'd roam the paddocks far and wide, and in the dam
    we'd swim.
Picked daffodils, oh what thrills for you and I, dear Jim.
There is much more, for I am sure those memories bring
    me back,
To another time, when you and I, good times we did not lack.

I still can hear that chainsaw roar, when Dad he cut the wood,
The splinters flew, the sawdust grew, and we thought it good.
But at the well, to us he'll tell, 'Stay away, you could fall in,'
We never dared, but only stared, so this was not a sin.

Remember when a storm would come, and make our
   Nana frown?
With lightning blue, and thunder too, she'd pull the brown
   blinds down.
By firelight, and lamps at night, that old green wireless on,
Blue Hills brought sobs, not Mrs 'Obbs, those shows now all
   long gone.

And sometimes we would walk a mile or two across the land
Down to the creek, 'twas gold to seek, just panning with
   our hand.
Then down the cave, or to the grave, black death her awful fate,
Almost alone, we had no phone, just Bob, our faithful mate.

What about in wintertime? The muddy roads were fun,
With gumboots on, we'd skid along, behind the tractor run.
Those old stone walls at times were falls – but over we would go!
Adventures ours, while herding cows; do you remember so?

How quickly do the years go by, we're now both middle-aged,
With family too, for me and you, so much we have engaged.
Another one for you will come, a grandpa soon you'll be,
No greater joy, a girl or boy, a great-aunt that makes me.

This next milestone now in your life, today's a special one,
Blow candles out, dance and shout, eat cake, have lots of fun.
I'll finish now, but do allow me to send you this,
Hip Hip Hooray, Happy 60th Birthday! Much love, your
    sister Chris.

Green

I look upon this lovely scene, reflections mirrored in the stream,
A sanctuary of calm delight where all is safe, peaceful
   and bright.
I yearn to lay upon the hill, with arms outstretched and stay
   real still,
To fix my gaze upon the sky and watch the white clouds pass
   me by.

I'll drift into a perfect dream, as I surround myself with green
With eyes now closed, and for a while, let tranquil beauty
   me beguile.
No thoughts to disturb my peaceful time, a newfound
   freedom will be mine,
My cares and worries drift on by, my soul replenished as I lie.

My body with the earth as one, a new beginning has begun,
I'll cast aside my outer shell and build my inner strength
   as well.
Just like a butterfly I'll change, a metamorphic rearrange,
The rebirth of myself – I will emerge renewed to feel the thrill.

Arising refreshed and with a smile, I'll sit and ponder for
   a while,
About this place that I have found – it's solitude without
   a sound.
No greater gift could I ever find than this captured memory
   in my mind,
A glimpse of heaven I have seen while lying on the hill of green.

World Nude Gardening Day – Again

Today my garden I must work
But first I should take off my shirt,
My trousers and my underwear,
Until I'm standing here quite bare.

My clothes, you see, I must discard
Before I step into my yard,
It's Saturday, the first in May,
Therefore, it's World Nude Gardening Day.

Although I feel a little chill
Out in my garden I will till,
Mow the lawn, mulch the weeds
And in my veggie patch sow seeds.

I'll brave the weather, rain or shine
And when I've finished have a wine,
I'll tarry not, there's much to do
May even take a picture too.

So you can see what I have done
Except I won't show you my bum,
I'll even try my very best
To avoid photos of my bare breast.

I hear the kids say, 'Not again!
She's even nude out in the rain.'
But they don't really understand
I have no choice – this day is planned.

So now I send a hearty cheer
To other gardeners who are out here,
Like me, this day they will not miss
World Nude Gardening Day – we can't resist!

Raining In My Heart

I see you walking in the clouds above
Umbrella overhead, sweet music plays.
Reminding me of all we shared
Before you left, that fateful day.

Our life was one of harmony
Our family grown; it was time for us
To roam the world and see what life would bring
We made our plans, without worrying.

You kissed my cheek before you went
Promised you would not be long.
You took your brolly in case it rained
I never dreamed that would be the end.

The time ticked by, I thought you'd be back
Rain drizzled down the windowpane
I waited patiently for your return
Then heard that knock upon the door.

A look of horror must've crossed my face
Their sad expressions told it all.
'I'm sorry, ma'am, but we bear bad news
An accident claimed your husband's life.'

I stared at them in disbelief
'He's on his way, he should not be long.'
I saw the pity in their eyes.
'We're sorry, ma'am, we have to tell you this.

It happened while he crossed the road
A driver through the red light ran.
Your husband never stood a chance
He suffered not; we're sorry for your loss.'

My heart was torn that tragic day
I close my eyes, and still see you.
You are by me with every breath I take
Freely now my tears run down my face.

I know that if you could, you would return
Take me in your arms and hold me tight.
I stand outside and wait for you, my love,
And when I raise my eyes, a vision comes.

I see you walking in the clouds above
Umbrella overhead, sweet music plays.
Please come for me, I'll go with no regrets
And be with you in love's sweet melody.

Fire And Flood

Once again, I set my pen to write of flood and fire,
Events from different states I tell, with consequences dire.
A flood was first, some days ago, from torrential rain,
The Hunter Valley's river raised; its bank put under strain.

This fast and rushing water took all within its wake,
Left many people stranded too when riverbanks did break.
The water rose and flowed along, the land it would surround,
Houses flooded, children cried, pets and livestock drowned.

The wettest year, reporters said, as we all watched the news,
With pictures shown of heartbreak hell, and flood-affected roos.
But people will all rise again and rebuild what is lost,
And we'll all help however we can, no matter what the cost.

Today I heard about a town that's just been razed by fire,
With nothing left of stores and homes but a scorching pyre.
Historic buildings all are lost, the school and hospital
Grapevines and olive groves are ash, the church no obstacle.

No letters will go out this week, the post office it did scoop
Some people missing, not yet found, from this town Yarloop.
The fireballs came, not one, but many soon thereafter
This lovely milling town all burnt by fiery disaster.

And as I sit and type away to tell you of these tales
My thoughts and prayers go to Yarloop and those in New
    South Wales.
But our Aussie spirit's so alive, it'll come now to the fore
And help soon given, best wishes sent, for these we'll not ignore.

Camp Inspector

There was movement in the campsite
for the word had passed around,
Camp Inspector Greg was on his way.
He was known from far and wide for his nitpicky ways
not even crumbs in toasters could they stay.

The tents attached to cabins were inspected one by one,
if sleeping bags were on the ground and not rolled up,
    · he wrote.
Or if the window flaps were up, or tent pegs not down firm
he smiled with glee, and points he took for each and every one.

First in Cabin One he went, inspecting all the beds,
he checked for wrinkles, lumps and bugs,
    and overhanging sheets.
With shower curtain pulled real tight, they thought they
    had it won
but then, alas, upon the floor he spied a tiny crumb.

He raised his hands, their hopes were dashed
from ten points he took off four.
'Now let this be a lesson, boys,
I'll not tolerate filth upon the floor.'

He quickly moved to Cabin Two, the girls had this down pat
all shiny was their kitchen sink, no wrinkles in their beds.
But then inside the dunny, he cried out in great delight
'This seat is up, you've lost your points!
Oh, what an awful sight.'

Cabin Three was next in line, he knew he had them licked
in every nook and cranny had a peep.
'Disgraceful, lads, it's like a sty – a pig would love this place!
I'll give you three, and hope next day
you'll see a smile upon my face.'

And then he strolled to Cabin Four, outside it he did stand
he gazed inside the windowpane, and then held up his hand.
'I can't see anything inside, the curtains here are closed
for that you lose eight of your points;
no further need I go.'

So last of all was Cabin Five, where his wife with some
    girls stayed
'Inspection's on, now let me see what I can find that's wrong.'
He walked and poked, he peeped inside, he even lifted lids,
but naught he found – completely right
at last, some tidy kids.

He shook their hands and kissed each cheek, 'No points I'll
    take away
you've done us proud – it's a perfect ten – with you, my dear,
    I'll stay.'
And to this day resides with one who never gives him strife,
his house is always tidy and clean,
thanks to his darling wife.

Black Dog

I have a raging storm inside my head
Black as a dog, clouds roll by without end.
A warning flash of lightning is my dread
Another surge of dark thoughts will descend.

I feel deep rumblings start, and then I know
Relentless raindrops form behind my eyes.
This black dog in my mind begin to grow
As flooded plains of anger start to rise.

A heavy heart and mind that won't abate
This void I can't explain consumes my life.
I feel I've lost my soul and it's too late
To claw my way out from this awful strife.

Flood tides creep in, until I start to drown
Deep breaths inhaled to calm this savage sea.
These black dog thoughts have kept me down
I think I need someone to rescue me.

I cower under covers like a child
Block out my ears and hum a simple tune
To try and stop my fears from running wild
I pray this hurricane will settle soon.

I see a glimpse of hope within my sight
My restless thoughts can find the peace I need
If I stay true to who I am and fight
With determined strength, I will succeed.

At last this storm begins to leave my mind
My sanity returns; my thoughts are clear.
But somewhere in my headspace I will find
This black dog is often lurking near.

Sweet Dreams

'No, don't wake him – let him sleep,'
the giraffe said to the dog.
'Do not disturb his peaceful rest
let dreams keep him agog.

In another world where there's no harm
no beating will he get.
There he can feel really safe
and this hurtful day forget.

Let's take him on a journey now
his dreams we will invade.
Lift him gently through his mind
let all his worries fade.

There he'll be just wild and free
he'll run and shout out loud.
In a life of fun and joy
with dreams of peace allowed.

Where people smile and never frown
good deeds are done with love.
Where boys can feel quite safe and sound
and there is no push or shove.

So let this night be just for him
keep stardust in his eyes.
Where he can dream of happiness
before he then must rise.

His waking hours bring no joy
filled instead with raw despair.
They are no fun for such a boy
who has no-one to care.

Instead, they beat him for his wrongs
and say he's never right.
For him, it seems, there's no escape
except in sleep at night.

Sweet dreams allow him to be free
amongst the purple skies.
With his friends, like you and me –
with us, he never cries.

So let him sleep, don't wake him now
his dreams must be his own.
And we'll protect and comfort him
so he is not alone.'

Bugger All

No broom you'll find in my hand
no beds are made or dishes done.
It's time to have my day off
today I'm doing bugger all.

I can't be bothered getting dressed
stay in my nightgown, slippers too.
The TV's on, I'll watch the shows
and all day long do bugger all.

Relax, today, I'll read a book
or stretch out in a big lounge chair.
I won't feel guilty doing naught
Instead enjoy just bugger all.

I'll probably have a nana nap
for meals, send out for takeaway.
Crawl back into my unmade bed
worn out from doing bugger all.

'Cause every other day I work
I cook and clean and sweep the floor.
Do the washing, walk the dog
no time at all for bugger all.

The most I'll do is hold my pen
to write this poem on the page.
I'll wonder if there's others too
just doing bugger all.

Second Time

Above the clouds, beyond the blue
You are, but in my heart you stay.
The stars shine bright, reflecting you,
Without a word you went away.
Your heart it stopped, through with life
Broke the bond we'd held for years.
My grief so raw, I balanced on a knife,
Tired of living life through tears.
But someone revived my broken heart
Restored my soul, so I could love again.
And with him I began a brand-new start,
His love replacing all my lonely pain.

On my left hand, two wedding bands I wear
One new, one old; with both, my love I'll share.

Gotta Go

Now, have you ever been 'caught short'
While traffic-jammed, and can do naught?
You feel the rumble, then you know
In that instant, you've gotta go.

The traffic lights, they all are red,
You play a game inside your head.
And just sit still and hold on tight
The urge to go you'll have to fight.

Sweat then begins upon your brow,
Oh God, you need to go right now.
You shift around, then with a squeak
Will mention that a loo you seek.

There's one you know that is not far
But then you are stuck in a car.
The traffic lights are still not green,
You sit and squirm and nearly scream.

You clench your butt, and feel the pain
'Please hurry up,' you do complain.
Distract your mind, try not to think
That you are really on the brink.

Leg muscles tense, you sit real still
And fight the urge with all your will.
A fart right now you must rescind
If done, all will go with the wind.

The only thing's to concentrate
If you do this, it might abate.
But no, by now your bum's on fire
For you, there's only one desire.

At last, the traffic starts to thin
The toilet's now your grasp within.
You whisper, 'Hurry, don't go slow
Get a move on, go, man, go!'

To the roadhouse, turn down the drive
Yes, finally, you do arrive.
With no more waiting, find the loo
Relief at last this is for you.

Back in the car, you grin then say
'A real close call that was today
No time to spare, I made it, though
When you've gotta go, you've gotta go.'

I see you smile at what I write
Cause you've been there, I bet I'm right.

Shiny Stiletto Heels

There's nothing like some gorgeous shoes
to compliment outfits you choose.
My favourites are stiletto heels
with a short skirt – so much reveals.

Six inches high and pencil-thin
so fun and sexy to step in.
A shiny patent leather pair
really nothing can compare.

When you walk in them, you must strut
from side to side just swing your butt.
And make sure to stand up tall
'cause if you wobble you could fall.

So practice first to get it right
once mastered, they'll bring much delight.
You'll capture everybody's eye
they'll look for sure as you stride by.

But once you're home, inside the door
you'll take them off – that is for sure.
Rub your toes, massage your feet
Put on your slippers as a treat.

Yes, vanity can be a curse
strutting your stuff is comfort adverse.
But my stilettos I shall wear
They're my favourites still, I do declare.

Beware The Witch's Spell

'Hey, look there, Jim,' the young girl said.
'What's this old gate up ahead?
Do you think we should go through?
I am game if you are too.

We'll have to clear these sticks away
and find the latch – what's that you say?
You don't think we should touch the gate?
What lies beyond might not be great?

Oh come on, Jim, don't be a wuss
all it needs is one big push.
Then once we're through, we'll walk the road
it's just your mind in overload.'

And as they heaved, the gate it fell
releasing then the witch's spell.
A curse held bound until the day
this gate was opened by its prey.

But these two children did not see
what dangers lurked, when innocently,
without a care stepped through the gate
and with this action sealed their fate.

At first, they heard a rumbling sound
as swirling winds whipped all around,
they both were lifted up on high
and drawn so quickly through the sky.

With a thud they were set down
inside a castle dark and brown.
Both trembling, cold, and full of fear,
'Jim, what has happened? Now we're here.'

A voice they heard; a cackle low
the witch appeared to let them know
they'd live with her forever more
no going back to life before.

'Your days will now be full of toil
you'll cook and scrub, the cauldron boil.
Oh, how I've waited for this day
when foolish kids would come my way.'

The girl said, 'Jim, I should've heard
the warning in your spoken word:
don't touch that gate, just let it be –
I wish I'd listened to your plea.'

A tear rolled down her cheek, then fell
upon the witch and broke her spell,
for witches cannot deal with tears
if splashed with one, their spell will clear.

And with a whoosh, away they went
back to that place were quickly sent,
behind that gate, set upon the ground
they both stood up and looked around.

'Where have we been? I can't recall
but know that gate must never fall,
so quickly we must go away
I'll not go through it on this day.'

So, if you see a gate ahead
be careful now before you tread,
take care with life and gates you fell
don't end up in the witch's spell.

To Be Or Not To Be?

There was movement in our government
For the word had passed around,
Those sitting pollies had to watch their seats.
Our constitution laws were passed many years ago,
To be a true-blue Aussie must now meet.
You cannot run for government, nor take a senate seat
If found belonging to another land.
So many now were hunting out their origins of birth
Finding DNA's another brand.

This all began now with our Bill
When Malcolm called him out,
'Stand up and show your papers to us, mate.'
But Bill just smirked a cunning smile, 'This time, Mal,
   you won't win
I'm a verified Australian,' he did shout.
However, Bill sought revenge, he raised the question up:
'Who among your ranks, Mal, do you hide?'
So when this rolling ball began, our pollies dropped like flies,
If not an Aussie, they were shoved aside.

Not one was safe from this turmoil
Even Barnaby was rolled,
A truer Aussie one could never find.
But by birth a Kiwi born, and so he had to go
Despite a big majority when polled.

Fiona from the Nationals next, One Nations lost its Mal
And Scott could not tree-hug – he left the Greens.
Larissa soon she followed, and Steven Parry too
Even presidents had to leave the scene.

Our sportsmen they were not exempt
Poor Alexander fell,
This time his serve was a double fault.
And so, the list went on and on, they vanished before our eyes,
The latest Jacqui Lambie's Scottish malt.
I really think this is a joke, and we must stop this rot
Like most Australians I have had enough.
Both sides play dirty politics, but need to count the stock
It's getting out of hand and far too rough.

Just do what you're elected for
And run our government,
For this mandate is what we all expect.
Remember what we stand up for; give everyone 'fair go,'
And if you do, you may gain my respect.
Because I'm disillusioned now, and feel I may migrate
To get away from all this bloody fuss.
If voting were tomorrow, not sure who I would pick
Perhaps I should run? Yes, this I will discuss.

The Kiss

They sat in silence without a word
Each in thought that was their own.
No spark of joy upon their face
These two old people, their story unknown.

As I gazed upon this scene
I wondered what they'd done before.
Was love still resting in their hearts?
Buried deep, afraid to rise?

His stare was blank, no recognition
And she just looked around the room.
No conversation or hinted smiles
How did they get to where they were?

With time, does closeness fade away?
Replaced with coldness, too afraid
To touch each other's hands?
Is this how it's supposed to be?

Then I looked away, and back
I saw him reach and kiss her cheek.
A little giggle from her lips escaped
My faith restored; love still exists.

I Am An Oxymoron

I think I am an oxymoron
quite different but the same.
Understanding less is more
subdued, yet can't be tamed.

I'll split in two while being whole
ditzy and still brainy.
Make many plans without a goal
be sad while being zany.

Have champagne taste with beery purse
find ugly very pretty.
Feel really blessed that I'm so cursed
quite stupid when I'm witty.

You see, there's more than one of me
sometimes I'm up when down.
Politely rude when wrong but right
show then a smiling frown.

Clearly confused, I know I am
more forward than behind.
Get close to you while staying free
be stingy when I'm kind.

Loud silence lets me contemplate
and dream when I'm awake.
To keep in front, I must backdate
my words, just give or take.

The Ballad Of Silly Sam

This ballad tells of Silly Sam
who thought Corona was a sham.
A non-believer who, when asked,
said, 'No, I will not wear a mask.'

He really thought he was immune
but would learn a lesson soon.
Defied the rules, the die was cast,
shouting loud, 'I'll wear no mask.'

Would not stay home while in lockdown
instead went out about in town.
'I know my rights, in case you ask
you cannot make me wear a mask.'

Sam would not listen to advice
and eventually, he'd pay the price.
His arrogance would flabbergast
'I will refuse to wear a mask.'

And then one morn when he awoke
his throat was sore, he thought he'd choke.
He found it hard to breathe and gasped,
'Perhaps I should've worn a mask?'

To the doctor's office he next went,
where swabs were taken and then sent.
Sam coughed and spluttered and finally asked
'Doc, please will you give me a mask?'

A hospital he was sent to
they put him in the ICU.
To save his life for them the task
he couldn't breathe without a mask.

But the virus took too strong a hold,
his friends and family were all told,
'Today, we think, will be his last.'
Their tears ran down inside their masks.

They watched as Sam took his last breath
this virus led him to his death.
They wailed as he lay in a cask
'If only he had worn a mask!'

Valentine Blues

Dear Valentine of my heart, please don't tear us both apart
I feel your yearning to be free, and hope that you will
    stay with me.
I love you more and more each day, but fear you'll take
    yourself away
I've tried to right this awful wrong, because with me you
    do belong.

You've never seen my silent tears, which I have shed for
    many years
And I can see you want to go, to be with her, yes that I know.
But for your love I'll surely fight, and if you stay, I'll make
    it right
Please don't break my heart in two; I never would get over you.

I don't know why with me you stay – perhaps it's guilt because
    you stray,
And you must think that I'm naive when you go out and
    then deceive.
But I'll stand by no matter what; just take a look at what
    you've got
A heart and soul that love you dear and are so thankful when
    you're near.

We were so happy and in love, the day we wed gave
   thanks above,
But o'er the years your roving eyes have caused me pain,
   now with your lies.
Each Valentine, it's me you kiss, but I know who you
   truly miss,
And so, although you're torn in two, I'm glad it's me who
   you turn to.

I know at times you try real hard to make it right,
   stop this façade
And in those moments, I cherish you, and pray that you
   will love me true.
Your indiscretions I'll forgive, for if you left, I couldn't live.
And maybe soon, you'll realise your Valentine's before
   your eyes.

The Keeper

Majestic lighthouse still you stand
Foundations deep beneath the sand.
With granite blocks and tapered tower
Uniquely structured staying power.

First you shone from burning coal
Next Argand lamps were fuelled by oil.
The mantle-covered flames shone bright
Before the steamed electric light.

At dusk, the keeper walked the stairs
Along the way each window checked.
With watchful eyes, the ocean scanned
Routes for those that crossed he planned.

The lighthouse keeper he did sit
Ensuring beacon lamps were lit.
Kept flashing signals through the night
To guide the sailors in his sight.

From dusk to dawn, bright signals sent
Light shone through thick optical lens.
During the day, this lens was cleaned
So through the night the lighthouse beamed.

For centuries, this system worked
A keeper's duty never shirked.
In any weather, they worked hard
Risking their lives without regard.

The ships that passed, their whistles blew
Alerted the keeper so he knew
Safe passage through, the rocks avoid
Their navigation skills employed.

The sailors would on him depend
For their lives he would defend.
But modern days see this decline
And rarely now do keepers climb.

For automatic eyes now sweep
No longer need man a man to keep.
Yet stately do lighthouses stand
Like empty shells across the land.

Many stories could be told
From memories lighthouses hold.
Of battles won and lost at sea
That only their keepers' eyes could see.

Childhood Ablutions

A picture of a little shed
reminds me of my old homestead.
The outhouse built within the yard,
a place no-one could disregard.

For when ablutions called you there
inside you went without fanfare.
No running water, or pull chain
a wooden lid that smells contain.

Upon the wall, pushed on a hook
newspaper squares when finished took.
No Sorbent soft, or thick four-ply
with just the paper you would dry.

And if at night-time nature called,
before you dashed, you often stalled.
To check for sounds or ghosts alike
then quickly ran into that dike.

When summer season came around
guess where the blowflies could be found?
And redback spiders were a threat
before you sat, you'd always check.

Then once we filled the dunny can
To bury contents was the plan.
But if you lived within the town
the night-man he would come around.

Yes, folks these days remember well
the outback thunderbox and smell.
The flies, the paper, running scared,
childhood ablutions now have shared.

If I evoked your memories too
when going to the outside loo
I'm glad you've stayed until the end
to read this poem I have penned.

Time Is Nigh

Two things in life we can't deny:
No choice in when we're born or die.
The hands of time tick steadily;
What we do between is key.

For some, their time is short, or not at all
Born into death, their life recalled.
Why is this so? Answers we won't find
The heartbreak left is so unkind.

Others survive, their journey starts
From many walks of life, whole worlds apart.
For some, wealth is always guaranteed
While others struggle endlessly in need.

Our choices made are ours alone;
No blame to others, when made we own.
The wise use their time to set the pace;
Fools who know no better, years they'll waste.

Time creates our greatest test
To make it count, we do our best.
So if your goals are incomplete,
Remember, time does not compete.

Our birth, our life, our death are set –
At different times, they must be met.
Clocks on the wall therefore remind
Our countdowns have all been defined.

Immortalised In Stone

He weeps while carving out her form
From memories of days past.
Their love was like a raging storm
In every weather so steadfast.

Together they had spent their lives
Carefree, no worries known.
He took her for his treasured wife
And she so took him for her own.

Entwined in love, a sweet caress
His fingers found a lump one day
'Twas in her breast; so with distress
A visit they the doctor paid.

'Bad news,' he said, 'the tests revealed
A cancer's grown, it's spread around.'
Her husband's shock was not concealed
No cure at this stage could be found.

In final days, filled with dread
They faced her death with heavy hearts
He vowed to her as tears were shed
Upon her death, they'd never part.

So from a piece of marble stone
Her form so perfect he designed
Her beauty to the world was shown
By this monument he'd leave behind.

This story happened years ago
She never left once she was formed
For all who see her now will know
Within her sculpture, love transformed.

Camp La-Di-Da

Have you ever camped with friends the rough and ready way?
With just a tent and sleeping bag, no mattress on which to lay.
When you find that nature calls, the shovel you then take
To dig a hole, and once you've done, the dirt and leaves
    must rake.

A billy-wash to keep you clean, no running water near,
The dirt and grime smear around, the smells sometimes
    you fear.
Cook a sausage for your tea, no fancy French cuisines
A bit of bread with sauce also, or maybe choose baked beans.

Yes, I have been to such a camp, many years ago,
But things have changed quite a lot, to Camp La-Di-Da
    we go.
Our set-up really has advanced, each year we add some more
Ablutions now in privacy – this we all adore.

A toilet tent erected fast, quite fancy, might I say
A short walk finds it out the back, for any time of day.
We even have a toilet seat, a bowl and paper too,
With just a flush of water, the waste goes down the loo.

A shower bay is all set up, with water cold and hot,
Design unique with taps and hose, it really has the lot.
However, though, there is one thing this shower really lacks
So, for next year, can we have our towels on heated racks?

Perhaps a movie theatre too, the footy we could see,
A waiter who could pour our drinks, a maid to cook the tea.
But I can wait for those things to come; I know it won't be long
Before Camp La-Di-Da lifts her game, I'm rarely ever wrong.

For some their tent has been surpassed, have a camper
    trailer now,
And spacious tents and mattresses, for others do allow
To sleep in soundly, snug and warm, while some an early rise,
'Cause time has no importance here; each meet their
    own desires.

Our food supply is never short, a feast we now expect,
A veggie roast or juicy steak with pepper sauce select.
Each afternoon at four o'clock the nibbles will appear,
Kabana, cheese and biscuits too, sip a cruiser, wine, or beer.

An afternoon of Bocce thrills, the little ball is thrown,
Amongst the leaves and sticks it's laid, the winner yet unknown.
Big silver ball now tossed by us towards that hidden one,
The closest to it gets the point; the winner shouts, 'I've won!'

Fishing lines are cast quite far into the river stream,
A great big cod for us to eat is everybody's dream.
However, fishing's just for fun, a nibble here and there,
And if we never catch a thing, we really do not care.

To sit around and read a book, a magazine or two,
Or listen to the football is quite enough to do.
Our time's well spent doing naught; there is no work for us,
That's why we come to La-Di-Da, and never make a fuss.

The dogs come too, they run around, occasionally have a scruff,
But overall, there is no strife, a warning growl enough.
Explore our campsite with a sniff, come around then for a pat,
Well satisfied, they'll lay about, for food eat this or that.

Yes, Easter time is when we come to our Camp La-Di-Da,
The ambience sure is fine, I'd give it a five-star.
It's not the set-up tents or site that makes our camp so great,
But the friendship shared between us here, each we call a mate.

Nearly Perfect

I know I am not perfect now
but nearly bloody close,
if not for all my wrinkles
or my great long pointy nose.

My figure it is hourglass
except for cellulite,
and in my hair, you'll find no grey
if I have dyed it right.

My boobs they sit up perky
in my brand-new push-up bra,
and my skin is always glowing with
my menopause not far.

My bum looks really great in jeans
With the elastic-sided waist,
you'll never see my tuckshop arms
in sleeves always encased.

My 20/20 vision has
come down to number ten,
I need to put my glasses on
more often now than then.

My pearly whites live in a jar
I take them out each night,
I know I am not perfect still
but most things are just right.

When I look into a mirror
sometimes won't recognise,
that woman staring back at me
with crow's feet near her eyes.

I'd like to think I haven't changed
but if I tell the truth,
old age has crept upon my bod
that once was flushed with youth.

Wolf-whistles I still get sometimes
if mistaken for a girl,
but how it sets my heart alight
my lips with smiles they curl.

Oh yes, I'm not so perfect now
some changes I do see,
but I can't go back, I'll now accept
this is who I'm meant to be.

It's Always Some-One Else

Some-one, it seems, will make a call
but no-one takes the blame.
I'm sure there is some-one for all
yet no-one has a name.

If some-one says 'It-was-not-me'
and no-one will confess
some-one will say 'Just let it be'
no-one creates a mess.

But some-one-else will then step in
'I'm-not-the-one,' they'll sigh.
It's always some-one-else's sin
'I'm-not-the-one,' he'll cry.

The other-one, 'It-wasn't-us'
these two both take a stand.
And finger-pointing make a fuss
when he just raised his hand.

I think that every-one can see
it's no-one's fault at all.
There's no responsibility
when no-one makes a call.

We'll never know if no-one tells
some-one will never say.
'It's-not-me, blame some-one-else
I'm-not-the-one today.'

Astral Travelling

Some nights I leave my body
and let my spirit fly
way out above the universe
looking down as I go by.

I visit many continents
and walk among strange crowds,
what pleasures do I come across
when freedom is allowed?

I soar through many cities
with arms outstretched I glide,
my body feels so weightless
all worries left behind.

The colours of the world I see
a kaleidoscope of lights,
I relish in the energy
enjoying all the sights.

The stars I touch, the moon caress
then back to earth swoop down,
fly back into my bodily shell
this flight I must adjourn.

But then, I know, another night
I'll fly away once more,
drift up again, release my soul
and let my spirit soar.

The Legend Of The Snowy River Ride

The man from Snowy River is a legend far and wide,
Who's known throughout Australia for his daring
   mountain ride.

From the station homestead, Regret's colt had got away
And joined the wild bush horses, upon that fateful day.

So the bushmen they all gathered, and our Clancy took
   the lead,
No better horseman sat upon his steed.

Their horses were all pure and strong, except for one, it's said,
A weedy beast quite undersized, but he was mountain-bred.

Clancy said, 'Let's take him, for every man will count,
He'll hold his seat, upon the ridge; we'll need him at
   the mount.'

And so, they started riding, their stock whips cracked the pace,
But when they reached the mountainside, they saw the
   horses race

Down a scrubby slope that defied most riders' skill,
But the man from Snowy River raced his pony down the hill.

Through the scrub he sped along, over holes and rough
    flintstones,
Until he finally beat them, and they yielded, white with foam.

He turned their heads and slowly took them homeward bound
This daring rider's mountain feat would surely spread around.

Yes, at Mount Kosciuszko, Banjo's story is often heard
Of this wiry lad whose courage became a household word.

Sitting On A Hill

The older I get, the less I do care
About all the things that used to be there.
Not sure if I should, but I worry not
Whether others believe that I've lost the plot.

I get up each day and do my own thing
I don't question time, or what it may bring.
I like the routine I follow each day
Read my newspapers, to see what they say.

Some things I can't change, I won't even try
If not my concern, I'll let them go by.
Help when I'm needed, do favours for friends
Smile at a stranger, my list never ends.

Walk in bright sunshine, breathe in fresh air!
Smell the roses in bloom everywhere.
Sit on a hilltop, admire the view
Paddle a river, yes this I can do.

Look back on my life and what I have done
No changes I'd make; regrets I have none.
The people I've met and places I've been
Are all meant to be within my life's scheme.

My family I love, hold dear to my heart
And when my time ends, from them I'll depart.
However, today is my time to be
I'll waste not a minute, each hour set free.

Sibling Rivalry

Sibling rivalry's alive
It is the bug bear of my life.
'I'm the favourite!' 'No, you're not!'
Oh, for God's sake, stop this rot.
I favour no-one, treat you fair
But with each other you compare.
'Mum did this with me today
You didn't come,' I hear you say.

'She loves me more than she does you!'
I'm telling you, that is not true!
Sometimes I see you one-on-one
A special treat from your dear Mum.
But next time it will be another
It won't be you, instead your brother.

I know you think that it's just play,
Not meaning the nasty words you say.
But when your rivalry's not planned
Sometimes, things do get out of hand.
When feelings are hurt you've gone too far
And then upset your dear old Ma.

So listen closely, no debate
I want to set the record straight.
When everything is said and done,
I don't like any one of you – MUM.

Pearls Pearls Pearls

Reflected in pearls your thoughts reveal
Wistful sadness for a regretted past,
Decisions made in haste you can't conceal
Dreams of yours were never meant to last.

Upon a pedestal you were his queen
Those early days, you thought his love was true
But in the background, kept from you unseen
His cheating ways he covered up from you.

For gambling, wine and women he would lust
While only in name you were his wife
He showered you with gifts to earn your trust
Behind your back in secret plunged the knife.

He wooed you to his side with such conceit
Made promises he never meant to keep
But blinded by his charm and false deceit
Your innocent naivety was cheap.

Then realisation of his sinful ways
Brought you to bended knees in stricken grief
For your raw heartache he would surely pay
How dare he steal your soul, this common thief?

You set the trap, and watched with great delight
When he stumbled headlong into your net
The proof was yours, he'd never win this fight
Revenge is sweet; you'd make him pay his debt.

They say there's nothing like a woman scorned
He left with just the shirt upon his back
While in his pearls, you'll always be adorned
His wealth ensures there's nothing you'll lack.

So heed my story, all you wealthy men
Ensure your pearls are given with pure love
Do not deceive your woman, or you'll find
You may end up just like that man above.

Brynners Are Grinners

There were movements in old Melbourne town
for the word had passed around,
Geoff and Brynne were quickly on their way.
To celebrate their nuptials, no expense was spared for this
a lavish wedding planned for their big day.

I wish I could've been there with them
to wish them both good luck,
but just like you, I never made the list!
The cut-off point 500, I know they tried so hard
to have me there, but sadly I was missed.

For weeks we've read about this girl
Geoff's known her for some months,
and as she stands beside him, what a pair!
They stand out like no others; this couple has the lot
to look at them, yes one can only stare.

They met through mutual friends, it seems
their romance blossomed true,
he showered her with gifts to win her heart.
A modern fairy tale for us, like Beauty and the Beast
let neither death nor money see them part.

And so, for several years at least
their romance seemed liked heaven
with Brynne beside him, Geoffrey looked real grand.
But the cracks kept creeping in, with whispers here and there
till finally our Brynne did take a stand.

'You're a lying, cheating blaggard, Geoff
please pack your bags and go,
I won't be made a fool of anymore.'
So, Geoffrey tried to calm her down – 'Brynne, don't kick
    me out!'
But she just laughed and threw him out the door.

And now we watch and read about
his next romance unfolding,
another young blonde woman he has snared.
She dresses up to please him, although at times not much
and even hits the streets at night quite bare.

Oh, Geoffrey, you amuse me so
you are a real sly fox,
your money, now, for sure it couldn't be.
According to the papers, you haven't much of that
it just must be your charmed sinceity.

And so, to Brynne, I'll say just this:
escape you did in time,
no intention had our Geoff to stay with you.
And next time, if you're tempted, girl, a poor man is the pick
at least he may remain to you true blue.

Hot Sweat

Down to my gym I did go
lifted weights, did cardio.
Sweat broke out upon my brow
but surrender I would not allow
squats and lunges, biceps curled
overhead bar we all hurled.

More cardio, it puffed me out
then I heard the instructor shout,
'Grab your plates for shoulders, please!'
I near buckled at the knees.
'Down on your mat, crunches now
hold in your core, you know how.'

Then she said, 'The step we'll use,'
up and down, I near turned puce.
'Just one more time, then we'll stop.'
Oh, thank God! before I drop.
Cool down at last, finish time,
'Lay down long and stretch your spine.'

I could have stayed for a peaceful nap
for my energy it did sap.
But glad I am I've exercised
mind and body energised.
Put equipment back in place
for next time, reserve my place.

Ten Cent Bag

'Do you want a ten cent bag?'
I then replied, 'No I do not.'
I have so many in my car
that I've once again forgot.

No plastic bags are given out
to shoppers on the go,
instead we must supply our own
to save the earth, you know.

But if you fail to carry one
you now can buy them cloth;
of course, there is a tiny charge
that may incite your wrath.

Instead I'll carry all my goods
and hope they do not drop,
I wish I was an octopus
with many arms to wrap.

I'm sure the stores all grin with glee
when trolleys are filled high
and shoppers have too much to hold
so a new bag they must buy.

Their profit margins surely rise
those bags cause a healthy gain,
when we forget to bring our own
and are forced to buy again.

So next time when you go to shop
ensure a bag you take
'cause if you don't, the store for sure
will a ten cent profit make.

Handy Man

Yes, I have one who's rather handy
when in a fix, he's fine and dandy.
He has machines and lots of gear
in his mancave – you'll find him there.

Just out the back and in his shed
amongst his toys all carefully spread.
Around his workshop, he will toil
from dawn to dusk, and sometimes boil!

Then I'll hear him curse and swear
when out of plumb, or not quite square.
He'll throw a mighty hissy fit
will surely say, 'Oh, bugger it.'

Upon the shelves, there's tools around
and up the walls, some more are found.
In drawers are screws and many nails
he's even got a set of scales.

But if he thinks he needs some more
He'll go down to his favourite store.
When he returns, he'll try it out,
'Come look at this!' I'll hear him shout.

So, I will smile and say, 'That's nice,'
and leave him to play with his device.
He'll potter round in sawdust too
and if not nails, use sticky glue.

His woodwork and welding all on show
around the house, but this I know:
for any job that needs a plan,
I'll go to my dear handy man.

Wi-Fi Frustration

Technology is not my thing
I know it can be great,
but I don't seem to have the time
it gets me in a state.

I write replies to be polite
push send when I am done,
and when I think they're on their way
I lose each bloody one.

The internet is so damn slow
connections in and out,
I curse at my computer screen
and sometimes scream and shout.

'I don't have time to waste, you fool,
you drive me round the bend,
my patience now is wearing thin
just GO when I push send!'

I start again, replies I write
then keep my fingers crossed,
when finished, send them off to you
and pray that none get lost.

I hold my breath and wait a while
until I see the line,
that's sending them across wi-fi
thank God it's worked this time!

I know I should slow down a bit
it's patience that I need,
so I will try to take my time
and not rely on speed.

And if I do, I hope I'll find
some calmness; then I will
settle down, I swear to you,
I'll keep my cool… UNTIL!

The Call

Alone, she sat down in her chair
for weariness had overcome
her on that day.
She would close her eyes
for just a while
and refresh her tired soul.
But little did she know
when she settled back
into her chair, to some comfort gain,
she would hear the call.
Her time on earth this day would end
as death reached out to take her hand
and lead her through the door of life
into its unknown sanctuary.
A peaceful shell she left behind
no frown upon her face,
instead, a calm embrace.
They found her then that afternoon
no sign of anything wrong,
'Mum's asleep; we'll let her rest,'
but then realised she was gone
from her earthly existence.
Transformed from life to death,
so easily, and peacefully.
'Goodbye, our dearest Mum,'
they cried.

Gunna-Doer

No longer am I gunna be a gunna
instead, I'm gunna be a gunna-doer.
Myself I'll rearrange, and make a little change
for this I thank my dear departed brother.

He left this life some time ago,
I know he didn't want to quit.
This opened my eyes, and made me realise
that life's too short to laze around and sit.

Also, I know I've much to do
I'm gunna change my slothful ways.
For plans I've made, not linga any longa
instead will fill each hour so it pays.

The jigsaw puzzle I shall now complete,
and when it's finished, put it in a frame.
I'll not procrastinate, instead make a date
to finish jobs I've started – that's my claim.

I'm gunna keep the dates I say I'll make,
ensure to catch up with friends.
Gunna sit in the front seat, I will not be beat
find and tie up my loose ends.

I feel as if I have just woken up,
this call I know my brother sent.
'Just be a gunna-doer,' I hear him say,
'make sure every day's an event.'

And if you read this little verse of mine,
please think about the words I say.
Things you have missed on your bucket list
don't leave till tomorrow – do them today.

Blood Red Sky

There was movement on All Hallows' Eve
with stirrings all around,
The moon was full in the blood red sky
dark shadows came and went.

I wondered if I'd make it home
before the dead returned,
wishing I had a mask to wear
to fool them as I passed.

I don't know why I went so far
from home that awful night,
instead of being safe inside
I faced the ghosts and ghouls.

What was that noise? My ears pricked up
I heard a cackle low:
'She's over there, don't let her escape!'
And I saw the ugly, rotting crowd.

Quick! Run, you fool, you know the way
don't let them catch you up!
The moon was up to light my path
I turned and ran like mad.

I saw the witches zooming by
on broomsticks made of wood.
They zigzagged in and out the trees
as black cats ran around.

Just up the path I saw my door
but fumbled with the lock.
Before it turned, I felt a hand
my knees went very weak.

'Ha, you fool, I've got you now
tonight you join our world!'
I saw his grey decaying face
and then let out a scream.

Waking up, I realised
it'd been an awful dream.
'Twas then I heard a rapping sound
and giggling at my door.

Opening it, before me I saw
zombies, ghosts, and ghouls,
three witches who looked very mean,
all grinning up at me.

I rushed inside to find my jar
with lollies and some treats,
I would not trick, instead I gave
to each child standing there.

But when they left, I shut the door,
made sure to turn the key.
If you see a blood red sky
it's sure to be Halloween.

What Am I?

No matter how a man may run,
He'll never win the race with me.
Throughout his life, I am the one
Who'll rule his world and destiny.

I am the thing that conquers all,
Despite the way man plays the game.
I'll help him rise, then watch him fall,
But I will always stay the same.

I share my wealth with every man,
Who'll take my goods without return.
But some reach out a greedy hand,
And take much more than they have earned.

I do exist in every place,
I lay the road that man must follow.
My work is done without a trace,
Without my help, no life would grow.

My door is closed, there's no escape
Though man may search to find the key.
But in the end, his life I'll take
Nobody ever runs from me.

I am the only one who'll last,
No-one can ever take what's mine.
I am the future, present, past,
You know my name, for I am time!

Just Who Is Cat?

I wonder if our feline friend's
an alley or a stray?
Just slinking round and looking for
a mate with whom to play.

Mischiefs made and boundaries pushed
she plays havoc with the world,
she'll spring right up and with a hiss
unleash her claws uncurled.

Or is she just a Cheshire Cat
who keeps us in a spin?
While lapping up the lovely cream
she'll wear a secret grin.

Her oval eyes will glisten bright
whenever a foe is found,
and with her pen she steals your mind
with words that are profound.

I don't think she's a ragdoll breed
that lays about and dreams
instead, she's always on the go
a busy mind, it seems.

Her life is often in turmoil
so much she's had to face,
But her nine lives are never lost
she'll win each uphill race.

I rather fancy she's Siamese
a pedigree, of course
quite lithe and graceful, sleek and clean
but vocally has force.

She'll say her piece, just meow it out
then sit back for a pat
or stretch right out and purr away
she's such a clever cat.

A tabby puss or tortoiseshell
with many shades to see
her stripes and swirls and magic too
entice both you and me.

Her varied ways, creative styles
delightful just to read,
no other cat can match her charm
she's just a one-off breed.

Exciting Uncertainty

I love to walk upon the path of life
Each day a new adventure to behold.
Wake at dawn to greet the sun at rise
Stretch out my arms, a new day to embrace.

What will transpire through each passing hour?
With every breath, I enjoy this time,
Not wasting a precious second in regret
Instead striding forth, each moment I'll seize.

With every step, my footprints leave behind
A mark to signify where I've been.
Reminding those who come across my path
That I have also walked upon this earth.

To smell the sweet perfume sent out in spring
And let the summer sun warm up my soul.
I'll clutch the autumn leaves upon the ground
Before the winter's chill my fingers seek.

Bright starry night brings peaceful offerings
Reflective wonders canopy this earth,
Tranquillity and calm, these gift supreme
Be mine to claim a thankful recompense.

The dawn escapes through night-time's cloak of black
To bring her lighted beacon to our sight,
No one will know where destiny may lead
Uncertainty forever will prevail.

How quickly time escapes our clutching hands
Before we must transcend to where we came.
But I'll embrace each moment like the last
Be never wasteful; make each second count.

I Write

I write because I love it,
Creating words upon the page
Thoughts arise unexpected
Upon my mind's stage.

Linguistic gymnastics confuse me
I have no understanding at all
When poem or prose is confusing
I won't bother then to recall.

Some writers set high expectations
And set down very strict rules
With the P.C. person for authors
Ensuring you use the right tools.

Scrutinising words of the meter
Making sure of the syllable count
Rhymes must be true, and not near ones
If not, you are disqualified – out!

When readers engage with the writer
Their attention is captured by words
Imagined or real does not matter
If the interest to read has occurred.

I cannot be false or pretentious
To impress for the sake of reviews
If my words were hollow and thoughtless
I would feel disloyal to my muse.

I admire writers with prowess
Who can move my emotional state
With well-written stories or poems
From thought, worthy lines they create.

We all have particular skillsets
Many writers prefer a free style
While other use meter and rhyming
Does not matter – if good, they'll beguile.

So, before you criticise others
Please look at your own imperfections
Take a breath, consider the authors
Who all write by their own intellections.

Shawline Publishing Group Pty Ltd
www.shawlinepublishing.com.au

SHAWLINE
PUBLISHING
GROUP

More great Shawline titles can be found by scanning the QR code below.
New titles also available through Books@Home Pty Ltd.
Subscribe today at www.booksathome.com.au or scan the QR code below.